RESPONSES TO
SUFFERING
Yours and Mine

Loren Broadus

Chalice ☙ Press®
St. Louis, Missouri

All scripture quotations, unless otherwise indicated, are from the *New Revised Standard Version Bible,* copyright 1989, Division of Christian Education of the National Council of the Churches of Christ in the USA. Used by permission.

Cover photo: PhotoDisc
Cover design: Mike Foley
Interior design: Elizabeth Wright
Art direction: Michael Domínguez

This book is printed on acid-free, recycled paper.

Visit Chalice Press on the World Wide Web at
www.chalicepress.com

10 9 8 7 6 5 4 3 2 1   01 02 03 04 05 06

Library of Congress Cataloging–in–Publication Data

Broadus, Loren.
   Responses to suffering : yours and mine / by Loren Broadus.
     p.   cm.
   Includes bibliographical references.
   ISBN 0-8272-3222-5
   1. Suffering--Religious aspects--Christianity.   I. Title.
BT732.7 .B696 2001
248.8'6 – dc21   00-012574

Printed in the United States of America

RESPONSES TO SUFFERING

SUFFERING

Yours and Mine

Dedicated to Catherine
for all the shared labor, laughter, and love

Contents

Responses To Suffering:
Listening, Thinking, and Doing Compassion

Responses to Specific Instances of Suffering:
Alzheimer's Disease and Hospice

Preface

Larry Gelbart, lead writer for the television series *M*A*S*H*, wrote, "What you let yourself do after a while is allow yourself to do bad work, to put anything on the page no matter how much you embarrass yourself."

After the research for *Responses to Suffering* was completed, I wrote a first draft of this book. The ideas flowed in all directions. The main concern was to get the ideas on paper. Then I gave the manuscript to critics, telling them that nothing was sacred in the manuscript, so: (1) correct any errors in spelling or grammar, (2) recommend deleting sentences, paragraphs, and chapters, (3) rearrange chapters, and (4) suggest titles of chapters and make any suggestions that will help the reader become involved in the book.

After I gave the manuscript to the critics, I reread it. It was embarrassing. The people who read through the maze of material and made suggestions for changing the book included Catherine Broadus, Philip Broadus, Paul Crow, Colette Horan, Tom Shurling, Tanya Tyler, and the following students who took a course at Lexington Theological Seminary in which the manuscript was used as a text: Rebecca Z. Brown, James Brewer-Calvert, Frances H. Gay, John A. Gran, Guy McCombs, Derek Penwell, Jeffrey L. Smith, and Eddie Varnum. Dr. David Polk, my editor, led me through editing, rewriting, and rearranging the contents of the book. Kevin Phipps manipulated the content in the computer, improved the book design, and saved me hours of time. This writing is a collaborative effort. I thank all these people for the time they gave so that you, the reader, might understand the many ways that we respond to suffering and find some answers to the problems suffering presents to us when we and those we love suffer.

All people mentioned in this writing are real. However, some names have been changed to protect privacy. In those cases, first names are used. Other people's names are real. In those cases, both first and last names are used. Since all people mentioned (real names or not) represent a specific response to suffering, you may remember a person who responded that way, and it may be you.

All scriptural references are from the *New Revised Standard Version Bible.*

Introduction

Karen's Story

Karen was diagnosed with breast cancer and has continued to deal with the disease for the last several years. When asked to give advice for responding to those suffering, she did so. Before reading her suggestions born of experience, get to know Karen as a person. She did not let the frightening disease kill her spirit. She responded by doing something to help others. That is described elsewhere in this book.

After graduating from Lexington Theological Seminary, Karen entered the doctoral program at Vanderbilt University. While in that program, Karen was diagnosed with cancer. She wanted to teach in seminary, and this was a bigger setback than she could even know. After struggling with the disease for some time, Karen received news that the tumors were shrinking, so she "squealed, laughed, cried, danced, and said thank you to God about four thousand times." Karen also finished her last exam paper, completing that stage of the doctoral process.

"I've learned a lot of lessons, most of them difficult, through cancer...Here's the lesson for today: While there is much that is profound in suffering, there is nothing more profound than its relief. And that's the gospel, isn't it?"

Some of her friends stopped writing, visiting, or phoning Karen. This was a very difficult time for her. She expected and needed her friends' support, and some of these people got tired of "being there."

In the span of a few years, Karen had more challenges than anyone should have. While struggling with cancer and being diagnosed as terminal at one point, Karen prepared for final exams, wrote a dissertation, submitted a novel to a literary agent, maintained contact with some friends, dealt with the feelings caused by other friends who abandoned her, coauthored a book with three other women who had breast cancer, and lived through the trauma of a failed romantic relationship.

On May 16, 1996, Karen wrote, "It's hard for me to believe how much has changed in a year. I remember walking across campus last May while they were setting up for graduation and thinking, *This time next year I'll either have my Ph.D. or I'll be dead.*"

On September 17, 1996, she wrote, "Perhaps my biggest triumph of late has been making it to my 39th birthday on the 14th. A bunch of friends gathered to feed me dinner and laugh with me, and that was wonderful. I'm in a funny position about birthdays these days. While most people my age are mourning the loss of youth and the onset of middle age, I am exuberant that another year has passed and that I have aged one more year. As a woman in my support group says to people who tease her about her age, 'Hey, 40's one of my goals.'"

On May 15, 1997, Karen described a disturbing process. "I can't tell you how many résumés I've sent out in the past year— for teaching positions, for chaplaincies, for administrative positions. I've gotten some interviews at some good places but nothing comes of them…For a long time I wanted to pretend it wasn't so, but I think I have to face up to it…People find out about my cancer and they lose interest. None of my references tell them, but you know how people are: 'Hey, I know so-and-so at Vanderbilt.' Then they call them up and say, 'What about Karen Stroup?' and the person says, 'She's great, she's well thought of here, and she has cancer'…I know that has happened in a couple of instances, and it's driving me crazy."

In many different ways, Karen discovered that there is a lot of prejudice against people with cancer. Three months later, Karen raised the same theme: "I applied to just about every job that I was even semiqualified for over the last year and a half. I had several interviews but not one for a teaching position. Some friends suggest it's the cancer. They may be right, but those are the sort of things you never know for certain."

Karen accepted a position as pastor of Central Christian Church in Springfield, Tennessee. "I love my work at Central. I can say without qualification that I've been happier here than I've been at any job in my life."

The following wisdom came from letters she wrote to her friends. Some letters were addressed to "My dear friends." Other wisdom is from her response to my questionnaire.

In a letter dated March 18, 1995, Karen wrote: "First of all, the questionnaire assumed that my suffering is in the past. Of course, I've suffered before and recovered from it, but right now, in the midst of suffering, it's only *this* event/process that I can think of. So my thoughts come not from reflection about the past but the experience of the moment."

The following are some of the insights Karen has to share:

1. Never try to prepare a person for death at the expense of their hope. Don't kill their hope. Hope with them. Never refer to "the stark reality of your situation," especially if you are a physician. Be with the person where the suffering is, either in hope or despair. If a terminally ill person, for example, wants to believe until the moment she dies that God is going to miraculously cure her, how is it comforting to her to be told that she's living a pipe dream?
2. Never underestimate the power of prayer, especially when praying for a friend or family member. Let them know that you are praying for them. "What I want from you, my community spread far and wide, is prayer, prayer, and more prayer. Pray for a miracle and pray for it to happen now."
3. Write letters and cards and e-mail messages. "Your letters mean so much to me; they often make the difference between a bad day and a good one."
4. Support the suffering one in many different ways. "I cannot say how important your love has been to me, how it has sustained me and kept me hopeful."
5. Life is difficult, suffering is inevitable, and the "good times" are not to be taken for granted as the standard by which life is to be judged, but as moments to be seized, squeezed, and drunk deeply of when they arrive.

In a letter dated January 28, 1995, Karen wrote the following list of "some things I'd like for you to know as you go about caring for me":

1. I don't want you to feel guilty that you don't have cancer. I wouldn't wish this on anyone, and I'm glad that you don't have cancer. Don't feel guilty that deep down you're glad that if it has to be someone, it's me and not you. How could you feel otherwise?
2. Don't feel guilty if you can't be present with me in the way you'd like to be or the way you think is "right." I say this especially to you preacher types.
3. Don't feel that you can't tell me about the rough things going on in your life…What I need is authentic friendship, and that means a two-way street.
4. Don't feel that you have to talk to me only about cancer and only about me. Let me know what's happening to you. (Your good luck is not my bad luck.)
5. Don't bury me yet. Let's dream together; maybe I will beat this disease and live not only to tell about it, but to live some of those dreams.

December 12, 1996, Karen wrote, "Two years ago I'd just learned of the metastasis of my cancer, and a year ago I was doubtful that hormone therapy would work and was facing the quality of life versus quantity of life issue. It amazes me how much things can change. I am well, and I really didn't think I'd ever be able to say that."

Karen knows how to deal with suffering, both when she suffers and when others suffer.

+ + +

Karen's ways may not be your ways of responding to suffering. Suffering is never just a subject to be discussed. It is an experience to be interpreted, understood, and used to create a better life. Karen did not just *think* her ideas about responses to suffering would be helpful or intelligent; she wrote about her experiences. We are emotional as well as intellectual and spiritual beings. Life is a process directed by our feelings, our thoughts, and our understandings of God. Suffering is first an experience, then an accumulation of thoughts challenging us to become more than we have been. Examining how we respond to our own and others' suffering tells us something about ourselves. It also reveals how our particular culture affects us and how we respond to suffering. Reflecting on what others say and do helps us determine what is most helpful to us and to others. Then we can choose what we want to say and do when we are suffering instead of simply parroting the clichés of our culture.

If we care for a person, we cannot separate that person's suffering from our empathetic suffering. We suffer because he or she suffers. So our responses to suffering cannot be neatly categorized into your suffering and my suffering. We suffer together. Suffering demands a response.

The first section of this book is primarily about suffering. It describes some ways specific people have responded to their suffering. Trying to separate suffering from our responses to it is to deny the nature of suffering. The book is designed to help you think logically, reflect theologically, and respond emotionally in the presence of suffering.

To aid in this process, a questionnaire is presented. Following are some questions to which several hundred people responded. The results are scattered throughout the book. Answering the questions will help you identify what you think and feel about suffering. This will provide a context in which to evaluate your own and others' responses to suffering. After reading the book and reflecting on your experiences, it will be interesting to see if you have changed the way you think and feel about suffering. Then make your own list of helpful "Responses to Suffering: Yours and Mine."

1. How do you cope with suffering?
2. What could people who tried to help during your suffering have done better?
3. What did well-meaning people say or do that hurt you when you were suffering?
4. What did well-meaning people say or do that helped you when you were suffering?
5. Does God cause suffering?

6. Does God allow suffering?
7. Can God relieve suffering?
8. Have you experienced such relief?
9. How did suffering affect your religious faith?
10. Did your faith:
    a. sustain you during suffering?
    b. prepare you for suffering?
11. Does God use suffering to teach lessons of life? (Does God hurt to help?)
12. Was the silence of God during your suffering God's fault?
13. Do people suffer because they sin? (Does sin cause suffering?)
14. In one sentence, write the best advice one can give or the best act one can perform to help people who are suffering.

Suffering:
Yours and Mine

Chapter 1

Levels of Suffering

When our oldest son, Mark, was sixteen years old, he had a traumatic experience for a teenager.

"I need the car to go get a haircut," he announced.

I handed him the keys and watched him move quickly out the front door. It was Saturday. Catherine and I were watching a football game on television.

About an hour later, we heard the car tires screeching to a halt in the driveway. Then a car door slammed. Ten seconds later, the front door was yanked open and then slammed. Mark stomped through the living room. He headed straight for the bathroom. The bathroom door slammed. We heard the shower curtain slide open then closed. I looked at Catherine. She looked at me and nodded as if to say, "You take this one."

I waited about five minutes before rising to confront the situation. Walking into the bathroom, I noticed that Mark was behind the closed curtain, probably standing in the middle of the tub.

"Son, what's the problem?"

"I'm not coming out until it grows back."

That could create a problem since we had only one tub/shower in the house. Five of us used it daily.

"What happened?"

"He cut off all my hair. I look terrible!"

A bad haircut can be traumatic for an adolescent. Personal appearance is very important. Feeling ugly can be painful for most people, especially in a culture that spends billions of dollars

9

trying to look pretty. The need for approval is extreme for most people, and never more so than when they are at that awkward age when hormones are raging and antennas of sensitivity to the words and stares of others work overtime.

"What did Jane say about me?"

"Do you think George likes me?"

"I don't have a thing to wear."

"What did you think of my speech?"

"He cut off all my hair."

This kind of pain may not have a lasting effect on someone, but it hurts.

The first level of suffering hurts and may demand our total attention for a while, but it does not permanently scar us emotionally, physically, or spiritually. Although these experiences of pain may not mar us for life, they scar us for a while. This kind of suffering is usually assimilated appropriately and used as a lesson for life. We learn to live with disappointment and may even turn the pain into a victory. When we do not make the cheerleading team or the debate club, it is disappointing. The disappointment may dig deeply into our self-confidence. Although it may linger in our resentment stockpile for years, it does not kill our spirit for the remainder of our lives.

Yet one who is humiliated, laughed at, and made fun of during adolescence may become a violent person. Gavin de Becker, an authority on violence, tells us that 100 percent of serial killers were abused children, hurt either with violence, neglect, or humiliation.[1] They were abused either physically or emotionally. We do not always know whether the injury is life threatening or not to the teenager, or to the adult for that matter.

After reading the first draft of this book, a friend told me that I focused too much on the Holocaust, Hiroshima, abuse, and violence.

"You ignore the regular sufferings many of our friends experience," he said. Arthur told me that his son was not being treated fairly by the baseball coach and some of the players. His son had a better batting average than the person playing ahead of him on the Little League team. His son also had fewer errors than the first baseman. Every night Jimmy came home almost in tears because the coach had not put him in the game or the players had called him fat boy, lard butt, or some other cruel name that referred to his weight. Arthur was suffering; he could not do a thing about his son's problem except listen and care. Compounding the problem was that Jimmy had been taught that if you give your best and perform better than your competitor, you will be rewarded. He had also been taught that people are honest and fair and will "do the right thing." Jimmy's questions about the ethical issues were painful for Arthur.

"My heart aches to see Jimmy so sad," said Arthur. Both Jimmy and Arthur had many sleepless nights tossing and tumbling, worrying about how painful the next day was going to be for Jimmy. Hopefully, Jimmy will use this experience to adjust to life and become a successful person. Maybe he will be more sensitive to others' feelings. Arthur listened, shared his thoughts and feelings, and cared. This seemed to make a difference. Jimmy stayed with the team and learned from the experience.

David was an outstanding young man in many ways. He was intelligent, had a pleasing personality, and excelled in just about anything he tried. David married right after high school. A year later, he and his spouse became parents. David enrolled at the University of Florida. Because David's home was in Jacksonville, he commuted to school in Gainesville, where he had an apartment. The question of his family never came up with the young woman he dated. After several dates, she discovered he was married.

"I can't see you any more," she told David. She was hurt and disappointed that he could do such a thing to her and his wife and son.

"I have to see you. I love you and I need you," David pleaded, but to no avail. After an hour of discussion (more like begging), she agreed to see him one more time to help him deal with their breakup. They met on campus near Murphy Hall. David pleaded; Sarah did not change her mind. David reached into the glove compartment, took out a .45 caliber handgun and said, "I don't know what to do. I never really wanted anything that I couldn't have." He placed the gun in his mouth and pulled the trigger.

While growing up, David never learned that sometimes you try as hard as you can and still lose. He did not learn that you cannot have everything you want. David's response to suffering was to drag everyone near him into his suffering: lover, spouse, son, mother, father, and friends. This young man with so much promise began a romantic relationship with someone other than his spouse. From the beginning the relationship was doomed to hurt a lot of people. What appeared to be a first-level suffering turned out to be radical suffering for David.

What would seem to some to be a painful incident, to others is a traumatic experience. The pain is unbearable. Sometimes this is because one is not prepared to sacrifice for others and to do without what one wants. We take seriously the pain of adolescence and young adulthood, even though it is not usually life threatening to us or the young person. Recent school violence reminds us that we cannot always tell how much a person is hurting.

Frederick Buechner experienced what every parent fears, the feeling of helplessness when one's child is suffering. His most intense pain occurred when his daughter became anorexic. As Buechner explains,

> Young people crave to be free and independent. They crave also to be taken care of and safe. The dark magic of anorexia is that it satisfies both of these cravings at once. By not eating, you take your stand against the world that is telling you what to do and who to be. And by not eating you also make your body so much smaller, lighter, weaker that in effect it becomes a child's body again and the world flocks to your rescue.[2]

While his daughter starved herself to the point of death, Buechner could not do anything that made a difference. He could not fix it as most parents want to do. He wanted to heal her. She continued to starve herself. Buechner was so caught up in his daughter's life that he was in danger of physical and emotional collapse. He confessed:

> The only way I knew to be a father was to take care of her, as my father had been unable to take of me, to move heaven and earth if necessary to make her well,

and of course I couldn't do that. I didn't have either the wisdom or the power to make her well.[3]

The psychiatrist told him that he couldn't cure his daughter, to stop trying. She survived and saved both herself and her father. There is no suffering like the suffering of helplessness when someone we love hurts and we cannot fix it. In the introduction to Buechner's "The Dwarves in the Stable" Peter Hawkins explains:

He [Buechner] comes to emulate the "passionate restraint and hush" of a God who refuses to overpower, to save any of us from reality. Not knowing what disaster to expect as he enters his daughter's hospital room, he discovers instead the divine presence all around him: "God in his very stillness, holding his breath, loving her, loving us all, the only way he can without destroying us."[4]

A bad haircut is not in the same league with a daughter battling anorexia nervosa, but it hurts, just as all suffering hurts. Being rejected by a lover may not be an emotionally life-threatening situation for some people, but for others it is a killer.

Elie Wiesel gives us a clue to the problem in his novel *Twilight*. The setting is a clinic for people whose delusions spring from the Bible. A patient says:

There is suffering and there is suffering. Who is more odious than the man who laments a lost object in the presence of one who has lost a friend, or the man who complains of a trifle in the presence of one who is condemned to die? I am not suggesting you should not cry when you hurt. But if you cry only for yourself, your cry, in spite of its echo, will remain hollow. Without life, death would be meaningless. I repeat: what matters is not to cry for yourself, cry for others. And for me too.[5]

All suffering is serious for the one hurting. We should cry for each other, symbolically if not physically, regardless of the level of the suffering.

Chapter 2

Radical Suffering

Radical suffering is defined as anything that "assaults and degrades that about a person which makes her or him most human...Capacities for affection, enjoyment, hope, and desire are eroded by radical suffering."[1]

First, radical suffering attacks our need to control. The need to control is always with us. When we do not get what we want or someone we love is hurt, we want to make it right, to "kiss it and make it well." We need to make things happen, to correct the wrongs. Yet there are times when we cannot kiss it and make it stop hurting.

The summer of 1995, Catherine, my spouse, awakened one morning hurting all over her body. Her knees, ankles, toes, hands, fingers, wrists, elbows, shoulders, neck, back, and hips felt as if they were on fire. She could not move. She had been assaulted by chronic arthritis. Her doctor said that it was the most progressive case he had ever seen. Thereafter, each day began with my drawing a hot bath, helping Catherine to the tub, and waiting for her to soak until she could move parts of her body a little. Then I dressed her. That was not always helpful to her. She often said, "You have never been dressed until you have been dressed by soft-hands Broadus."

One day she looked down at her bra and said, "It's inside out."

"It works, doesn't it?" I reasoned.

She looked at the bra again and agreed that it was doing the job. Even in pain, she never lost her sense of humor.

The doctor prescribed one medication after another. Nothing seemed to help much. Finally, he prescribed a drug that would take six months to have an effect on the arthritis. Methotrexate, plaquenil, and prednisone finally gave her some relief.

For more than six months we were out of control. I could "kiss it," but I could not make the pain go away. I gave Catherine my love and support and helped bathe and dress her, which was helpful to her in some ways, but it did not diminish the extreme suffering. Radical suffering attacks our need to control. We feel powerless over suffering.

Second, radical suffering attacks our need for meaning. It threatens our need to believe in people: their decency, their goodness, their willingness to help in a crisis, and their capacity for compassion. An extreme case of radical suffering occurred in the Nazi Lagers, Hitler's prison camps.

Primo Levi describes how he and other prisoners were stripped of their dignity by:

- receiving irrational beatings for not understanding the German language,
- being stripped of their clothing and having all their bodily hair shaved off,
- living in filth with just enough food to survive,
- being tattooed with a number on the arm instead of being called by name, and
- not being given a spoon so that they would have to slurp their food like animals.

Levi writes:

Not by our will, cowardice, or fault, yet nonetheless we had lived for months and years at an animal level. Our days had been encumbered from dawn to dusk by hunger, fatigue, cold, and fear, and any space for reflection, reasoning, or experiencing emotions was wiped out. We endured filth, promiscuity, and destitution, suffering much less than we would have suffered from such things in normal life, because our moral yardstick had changed. Furthermore, all of us had stolen: in the kitchen, the factory, the camp, in short, from the others…We had forgotten our country and our culture, but also our family, our past, the future we had imagined for ourselves, because, like animals, we were confined to the present moment.[2]

Radical suffering may dehumanize us, causing us to lose our sense of worth, dignity, hope, and sometimes love. It threatens our belief in a world where people play fairly, live morally, cry sometimes, laugh a lot, enjoy intimate relationships, and know what to expect from most people. In radical suffering, there is not enough stability, predictability, and sameness about the people and the institutions with which we associate to help us feel secure and reasonably comfortable in the world. Radical suffering shatters emotional, social, and physical security.

One of the tragedies of radical suffering is the loss of identity. We lose the sense of who we are as workers, family members, friends, and spiritual beings with a relevant past and a touch of hope for the future. We are not who we have been in the past. We may have violated our moral code of conduct because of our suffering. This change in us may happen when we experience extreme suffering, but it does not have to. If people respond with care and compassion when we are suffering, our faith in people's goodness and concern and their altruistic drives will be affirmed and in fact increased.

Third, radical suffering attacks our belief in a God of compassion, in a God with the power to intervene in life's crises. We need a God who makes a difference in our lives and in our world. Radical suffering can rob us of the beliefs upon which we base our lives.

Rev. Charlotte W. felt the exhilaration of stepping into the pulpit to present her well-prepared speech to the people at the church assembly. The speech was scripturally and intellectually challenging, each point decorated with humorous incidents. After describing an incident in school about being hit with a spitball, the audience laughed. Then Rev. Charlotte's eyes narrowed and her shoulders lifted as she leaned over the pulpit, shot her right fist toward the people, and solemnly said, "Sometimes God uses pain to get our attention."A few minutes later I left the balcony. As I walked out of the sanctuary, Sally greeted me with, "Can you believe that Charlotte said that God uses pain to get our attention? I'm angry! How dare she blame God for George's cancer!" Sally's glaring eyes, clenched fists, and hostile tone suggested that she did not believe that God uses pain to elevate the divine ego.

Jane and David walked out of the sanctuary. David was embracing Jane's slumped body. Her head rested on David's chest as she sobbed. We walked outside to the churchyard. The three of us had been friends for years.

"My grandfather sexually abused me for years when I was a little girl," Jane confessed after regaining her composure. "It was horrible." After sobbing for another five minutes she said, "After hiding this for thirty years, I decided a few months ago to see a therapist to deal with it. It seems I'll never get over it. Oh!...It affects my sex life with David, my intimacy with my children, and...everybody and everything... When I begin to feel a little relief, I'm told that God used my grandfather's sexual abuse to get my attention!" The tears were from her soul, the pain from her childhood, and the fears were today's fears encompassing her past, present, and future.

Although Rev. Charlotte did not intend for her words to be used to condone child abuse or cancer, that's what Jane and Sally heard. "God sometimes uses pain to get our attention." God like a father? God like a grandfather?

Radical suffering attacks belief in a God of compassion, a God who can, and wants to, relieve our suffering. It tests our beliefs about people, God, and ourselves. Darrell Fasching wrote, "If God is to be God, it cannot be at the expense of human beings."[3] If we believe that God uses suffering to get our attention, and many Christians do, we have to justify the suffering while still believing in a God of love. That is not easy.

Fourth, radical suffering attacks our hope in a future worth living. Allen and Sue had been married thirty-nine years. As in all good marriages, Allen and Sue had gradually assumed different functional roles. Sue managed the day-to-day operation of the family—paying monthly bills, phoning to correct billing errors, making doctor's appointments for the children, and managing the interior of the house, deciding when and what needed repairing and painting. Allen specialized in investments, retirement programs, and yard and exterior house maintenance. Sue cooked. Allen washed dishes. Sue decided when and what medicine the children took. Allen decided when a cut foot or finger needed stitches and when an arm or leg needed to be x-rayed. Their experiences and skills, not gender, determined who did what.

Allen and Sue loved each other, respected each other, laughed often, cried rarely, and lived through life-threatening situations with each other. They supported each other while raising two children during the sixties and seventies.

Then Sue died. Allen was devastated. He did not know what to do or think or feel. He was lost not because of the bill paying or cooking or other functions Sue handled, but because of the absence of Sue. She was the presence in his life that helped him make sense of the world. Watching television alone was not the same; being with friends was not the same; eating alone left the food tasteless. When the shades of night signaled the end of another day, Sue's absence screamed in Allen's head and heart. Half asleep, he would roll over in bed expecting to wrap his arm around Sue's warm body. A cold sheet greeted his hopeful hand. Loneliness, anxiety, and anger filled his soul.

The future looked very bleak. Life was something he endured. He did not have any hope for joy or happiness of any kind. Depression dug deeply into his reasons for living. Radical suffering attacks our hope for a joyous future.

"In the depth of suffering people see themselves as abandoned and forsaken by everyone," claims the German theologian Dorothee Soelle.[4] Contrary to what Milan Kundera thought when he wrote, "In intense suffering the world disappears and each of us is alone with his suffering; suffering is the university of egocentrism,"[5] we do *not* have to suffer alone.

In summary, radical suffering threatens to make us less than we are as caring human beings by

- attacking our need to control, thus rendering us helpless,
- attacking our belief in people's capacity for compassion,
- attacking our need for a God who cares about us and helps us in times of suffering,

- attacking our hope for a life worth living, and perhaps
- increasing our sense of isolation and alienation.

Some people respond to these attacks by "giving in" to their suffering and becoming hopeless, depressed, angry people. Others discover an inner strength helping them become more than they thought they could be. The responses we get from other people when we are under the attack of radical suffering influences the way we handle the pain. The presence of a child, a mother, a father, other family members, a friend, or a pastor tells us that God is also present. We are not alone when suffering.

Chapter 3

No Pain, No Gain

On August 5, 1996, *Time* magazine described the following dramatic Olympic incident. When Kerri Strug took off down the runway late Tuesday afternoon, ignoring the intense pain in the left ankle she had sprained on her previous vault, she thought she needed "to stick it" in order to give the U.S. women the gold medal in the gymnastics team competition. Strug did more than win a gold medal. She added another word to the Olympic credo: *cities, altius, fortius, audacious*: faster, higher, stronger, braver.[1]

Jackie Joyner-Kersee made sports headlines when she jumped to a bronze medal on her last try. She had her leg heavily bandaged, as she was suffering from a severe hamstring injury. The greatest woman athlete in the world once again demonstrated her courage and capacity to endure pain.

We admire people who accept the pain to accomplish what they want. We make heroes out of them. We believe that enduring pain without complaining demonstrates character and shows what we are made of. Olympic athletes would not be competing if they could not stand pain. The thousands of hours of practice, the years of running, doing sit-ups, pumping iron, grimacing while squatting, jumping, and doing all sorts of exercises needed to develop the muscles required to run faster, jump higher, lift more, and do "it" while hurting is the price these athletes pay for their dream. Is it worth the gold to push the body to the point of exhaustion? Is it worth it to "play hurt"?

Some suffering is a by-product of the goals we set for ourselves. It is the result of a choice. We are constantly confronted with making choices that will cause suffering. Is it worth it to raise children? The pain we feel when they hurt is the price we pay for loving them. Is it worth neglecting our children to get ahead in the world, to become CEO of the firm? Is it worth the pain of daily exercise for some to be beautiful and others to be healthy? "No pain, no gain" is the slogan of many health spas. It is a cliché that contains some truth. Many things we want in life cost physical, emotional, and spiritual pain. Is it worth it?

The plumbing in our bathroom clogged. After my futile efforts to unclog the sink, we called a plumber. So that we would not have to pay this high-tech skilled worker again, I watched every move he made.

"How long have you been a plumber?"

"About a year," he replied.

Since he was middle-aged, I asked, "What did you do before you started plumbing?"

"I was in prison," he calmly said in the same voice he would have used if he had said he worked for McDonald's.

"What were you in prison for?"

"I killed a man. He deserved it. They gave me ten years." He said that in the same voice he would use to order a Big Mac. I thought this could be interesting.

"Who was the strangest person you met in prison?"

He put his wrench down, looked up at me, and said, "There was this man in there that read books and didn't have to. He was really strange. I stayed away from him."

I went downstairs and closed the door to my book-lined study. It had taken this plumber three years to pass the state plumbing examination. It was extremely painful for him to read. He spent scores of frustrating hours trying to remember all that "book stuff," as he called it. But he was willing to go through the agony of reading over and over again what he needed to remember until he reached his goal. He became a plumber. Suffering is sometimes the result of our choices.

I worked my way through college playing football at the University of Florida. The practices were painful. The games were painful. I used to fantasize about the summer, when my legs, arms, fingers, feet, shoulders, back, and head did not hurt. In the late forties, spring practice lasted most of the spring.

The pain was worth the reward. I received a college education. The education cost some broken bones, scores of bruises, a few blood clots, about a dozen stitches, a dislocated shoulder, and other physical injuries. But there was the formal classroom education with a degree. There were also experiential lessons of life. From the experience of playing on a football team, I learned:

- You pay a price for success.
- Sometimes when you try as hard as you can, you still lose.
- You have to keep trying even when losing.
- You must sacrifice for others. Sometimes you sacrifice your comfort for the good of the team by throwing your 155-pound body in front of a 255-pound man to prevent him from tackling the ball carrier.
- You do not give up when confronted by the first obstacle; you continue toward the goal. You pursue your goal even when the odds are against you.
- Exercise, diet, and sleep are essential to getting what you want, if that goal requires physical dexterity. Intense study filled with many sleepless nights and fourteen hours a day of work may be the price you pay for becoming a professional person.

Working my way though college by playing football was worth the pain, even though there are some cold nights when I wish there had been less physical ways to get my experiential and formal education.

D. H. Lawrence is best known as the author of *Lady Chatterley's Lover* and *Sons and Lovers*. This Englishman wrote poetry, essays, and fiction. Today, we praise his skill and think of him as a major literary figure in history. Lawrence wanted to be just that, but the road to his goal was hard. He was teaching school to earn money, which took time from his real love, writing. He decided to quit his job and devote all his time to writing. That was difficult to do because he wanted to eat and to sleep in a reasonably comfortable shelter. He did not earn enough money from writing to buy food. So Lawrence depended on the charity of family, friends, and his literary agent to support him. He drifted from one free lodging to another. His biographer wrote, "Now the Lawrences were homeless, and for the first time utterly dependent upon the charity of others."[2]

Moving from one gift of shelter to another, Lawrence wrote (in 1917 or 1918), "I sit in bed and look at the trees and learn songs from a book and wait for the judgment day."[3] Another time when he was depressed he wrote, "I feel absolutely run to earth, like a fox they have chased till it can't go any further, and doesn't know what to do. I don't know what to do nor how to go on: like a man pushing an empty barrow up an endless slope."[4] At a different time in his life he confessed, "I don't know how on earth we shall get through another winter."[5]

In the midst of begging, failing, and lacking the basic needs of life, such as food and shelter, Lawrence never tried to get a job. He could easily have found work. He was trained as a schoolmaster with experience as a teacher. He did not want to teach just to earn money to support him and his spouse. Lawrence paid the price to be a successful writer. It involved a lot of unnecessary suffering that did nothing to gain the respect or admiration of others. "No pain, no gain" seemed to be an excuse for Lawrence to indulge himself in the charity of others. Regardless of how it affected others, his narcissistic need to do what he wanted caused him to abuse his relationships with friends and family.

In some cases, our sacrifices to reach our goals require some pain to gain what we want and need. In other cases, "no pain, no gain" is a myth that seduces us into inflicting wounds on others and ourselves to become martyrs of suffering. In these situations, our suffering is the goal, not the goal we proclaim.

Sometimes suffering is a choice; but other times we are ambushed by agony.

Chapter 4

The Gift of Pain

When asked to list his attributes, linebacker Reggie Williams (then with the Cincinnati Bengals) said, "Speed, strength, and the ability to recognize pain immediately." In his humorous comment, Reggie describes a normal experience–the capacity to feel and to identify pain. Without the capacity to feel physical pain, Reggie could have maimed himself by playing on a broken ankle or with a crushed nerve in the neck. In this case, pain was a gift. Not all people feel physical pain.

Dr. Paul Brand worked for years in India with people who had leprosy. He witnessed the many ways lepers were injured because they did not feel the pain normally accompanying a broken ankle, a serious cut, or an ulcerated sore on the ball of their foot. He himself experienced what he calls "congenital indifference to pain."[1]

One of the problems lepers have is their inability to feel when they are in danger of hurting themselves seriously. Without such warnings they do not get the help needed to prevent compounding the problem. At one stage of the disease, people with leprosy lose the capacity to feel pain when they back into a hot stove, cut a finger, or slip and hit their head against the edge of the tub. They do not know there is a big gash in their head until they see the blood. They cannot feel the broken glass that cuts their finger while washing the dishes.

In *Pain: The Gift Nobody Wants,* Dr. Brand expresses his convictions about pain.

My thoughts about pain developed over many years as I worked with people who suffered from pain and

24

people who suffered from the lack of pain…I readily admit that my years of working among pain-deprived people have given me a skewed perspective. I now regard pain as one of the most remarkable design features of the human body. And if I could choose one gift for my leprosy patients, it would be the gift of pain.[2]

We do not usually think of pain as a gift. When we are in intense pain, we think of it as a curse, something to be avoided at all costs. It would be difficult to be fully human to others without the capacity to feel physical, emotional, and spiritual pain. Brand writes, "We cannot live well without pain, but how do we best live with it? Pain is a priceless, essential gift–of that I have no doubt. And yet only by learning to master pain can we keep it from mastering us."[3]

We do not master pain, as Brand contends. We learn to cope with it, and maybe learn and grow from it emotionally and spiritually. A description of a few characteristics of pain will help us understand this "gift that nobody wants."

First, pain demands our undivided attention. Writing from experience, Albert Camus claims, "Pain clings to the present; it calls for a struggle that keeps us busy."[4] Pain tries to keep us thinking about ourselves. Intense pain demands our total focus; it wants to be the center of attention. We personify pain, sometimes talking about it as if it were a pet, a child, or a close relative. "That pain will not go away; it just keeps gnawing at my stomach." "That demon still hurts me. Even at night, it won't let me alone." Pain tempts us to be narcissistic and ignore all that is going on around us. We want the painkiller at almost any price. After years of pain, Simone Weil, the mystic and masochistic "saint" wrote, "Physical pain and that alone has the power to claim our thoughts."[5]

In the novel *Sights Unseen*, Hattie Barnes, a twelve-year-old, describes growing up in a home with a mother who is manic-depressive (bipolar is the term most often used now for the disease). The mother is unpredictable and often unresponsive to Hattie's needs. When she is depressed, the mother is demanding, mean, and totally obsessed with her wants and needs. She may scream one minute and cry the next over simple things, such as someone laughing downstairs or talking too loudly. From the beginning, Hattie was doomed to feel her mother's rejection. Hattie's father told her that because her mother could not satisfy Hattie when she tried to nurse her in the hospital, her mother told the nurses not to bring the baby to her. "If I didn't need her, she didn't need me," she told Hattie's father.

Even as a child, Hattie thought, "If I had a daughter as needy for my love as I was hers, I could, I thought, will myself to be well for her sake." Hattie described the family scene:

> Mother was depressed almost always, and her sadness was fractured only by wild, delusional turns of mind, with brief periods of stability that were celebrated and remembered by my family as though they were spectacular occurrences, like total eclipses or meteor showers.[6]

Hattie lived in a home where her mother demanded to be the center of attention, not because she wanted to but because her depression demanded to be in charge of her moods and actions. It was as though the depression were always having a temper tantrum, crying out, "Look at me, I am in charge." Pain does that to people. It demands to be the center of attention.

Second, pain belongs to a particular place, time, and culture. We are taught how to respond to pain. We do not necessarily respond to and feel pain the same way others do. David Morris contends:

> Because we come to understand our pain only within specific cultures and subcultures, it seems quite fair to describe our experience as, to a large degree, learned…The typical Irishman learns to grit his teeth and keep silent. The Micronesian woman in labor gives so little evidence of pain that only by placing a hand on her abdomen can the visiting Western doctor know when a contraction occurs. Who can doubt that chronic pain involves patterns of learned behavior?[7]

As a freshman in high school, I was a running back on the football team. I was taught somehow or some way that it was not acceptable for me to complain about pain. So when my left hand was broken, I did not tell anyone. I played the season with a broken bone in my hand. The football subculture said that one was not supposed to complain about injuries, because everyone hurt every day. In that same high school, if one broke a hand while rehearsing for the school play or editing the school paper, the injury would probably be reported with grimacing, shouting, or screaming. The editor would probably get some sympathy, while the football player would be expected to "tough it out." Within the same culture, there are different ways to interpret and respond to suffering.

Paul Brand explains that in India the beggars in great need, some of them deformed with leprosy, "formed part of the urban landscape. The philosophy of Karma taught people to accept suffering; like weather it is an unavoidable part of fate."[8] In most parts of our culture in the United States, we think of pain as an aberration of nature instead of as an integral part of what we are as human beings.

The novel *Things Fall Apart* is about Africa, missionaries, and a culture that is different from what most people reading this book could imagine.[9] Okonkwo ruled his household with a heavy hand. His wives, especially the youngest, lived in perpetual fear of his fiery temper, and so did his little children. Perhaps down in his heart Okonkwo was not a cruel man. But his whole life was dominated by fear—the fear of failure and weakness. It was deeper and more intimate than the fear of evil and capricious gods and magic. It was greater than the fear of the forest and of the forces of nature, malevolent, red in tooth and claw. Okonkwo's fear was greater than these. It was not external, but lay deep within him. It was fear of himself, lest he should be found to resemble his father. As a little boy he resented his father's failure and weakness, and even now he suffered when he recalled how a playmate had told him that his father was *agbala*. That was how Okonkwo first came to know that *agbala* was only another name for a woman; it could also mean a man who had taken no title. And so Okonkwo was ruled by one passion—to hate everything that his father, Unoka, had loved. One of those things was gentleness, and another was idleness. In that culture, it was not acceptable for a man to act weak, so he lived with the pain caused by his fears and hostility.

The same drama takes place in our more "sophisticated" culture in the form of spouse abuse, child abuse, and other forbidden behaviors. Some learned responses to pain should be challenged. Is it helpful to continue in a relationship where I am expected to accept abuse as normal? NO! In these situations pain is not a helping gift; yet it still demands to be the center of attention. The victim asks, "How do I take charge of my life and exorcise this demon?" Sometimes we lose the battle and learn how to live with the demon, and sometimes we win our freedom with the help of medication, friends, physicians, therapists, and God.

Chapter 5

Fear as Suffering

All people suffer from fear sometimes. Some people suffer from fear most of the time. And some live in constant fear of someone or something. There is the fear that gnaws at some, hour after hour, day after day, week after week. One may be afraid of failing, being ridiculed by a boss, being rejected by a lover or family, or being criticized by a friend. Fears such as these eat away at one's sense of well-being and one's emotional security and confidence.

There are those who are afraid some of the time of some things or someone. They may be afraid of growing old, being hit by speeding cars in heavy traffic, "sounding dumb" because of the questions they ask in a meeting, having a heart attack, or dealing with loud, boisterous people, but they live normal lives. Fear is a fact of life with which we have to deal. The suffering questionnaire asked people, "List the best advice one can give to people suffering." One respondent wrote, "Admit and give away your fear." It may not be that simple. So now we will examine fear.

1. *Fear has to do with the future.* It is a feeling caused by a thought. We think we might be hurt in some way, and it scares us. We might have an automobile wreck, get seriously ill, lose our hair, or...You fill in the blank. We may be afraid that

- In retirement we will live in poverty.
- We will be attacked in the mall parking lot.
- We will suffer with cancer, just as our mother did.

- We will become an alcoholic, just like our father.
- We will marry an abusive spouse or become a spouse abuser.
- Jane will say no to our marriage proposal.
- Nobody will ask us to the senior prom.
- We will have to live alone for the remainder of our lives.
- Our child will be born with a defect, either physical or mental.
- We will be fired after working twenty years for the same company, and management will call it downsizing. No pay, no pension!

2. *We learn what to fear.* When we are children, we learn what to fear from our parents, our peers, other adults, television, computer games, and other sources. We are taught to be afraid of some things or people to protect us from getting hurt. As a child I was told: Don't play with matches; don't go within one block of the river; don't run across the street; and don't play in the street. These mandates were warnings of danger and possible pain. We learn to fear other things or people through experience. We visit a friend or loved one in a nursing home and say, "I sure hope I'm never in that condition." Some people are afraid they will become totally helpless one day. A car slammed into the rear of our car on a rainy, slick highway in Winston-Salem, North Carolina. Now every time it starts raining on an interstate highway the anxiety rises; the muscles tighten in my neck and arms. Even Mom's Motel looks good to me in such times. An abusive parent makes us afraid of people. We are not talking about reason; we are talking about emotional and physical reflexes.

Just about anything can be a source of fear. The June 9, 1998 issue of the *Lexington Herald-Leader* newspaper had an article on phobias. It listed the objects of people's fears: dogs, horses, spiders, snakes, flying, heights, enclosed places, dentists, the number 13, being alone, crowds, cats, and sharp objects.

Fear of rejection is one of the most prevalent fears: the fear that we are not dressed properly, do not look as we should, do not speak in an acceptable manner, or fail to fit into our group in some way.

Fear of public speaking is common. In college, a classmate asked me to help him in a speech class. Although he was a tackle on the University of Florida's football team, six feet eight inches tall, weighing about 270 pounds, he was petrified of giving a five-minute speech. I thought, *I wonder what he thinks they are going to do to him.* It did not make sense to me at the time. Of course, he was afraid of embarrassing himself. Many fears do not make sense, but that does not mean the fear is any less real or painful. As one reviewer reported, "My sister's college roommate was afraid of feathers to the point of getting hysterical when she saw one. Apparently, as a child, ducks or geese attacked her, and feathers sparked that repressed memory."

All fears are not created equal. Fear resulting from date rape does not feel like the fear one has when thinking about missing the senior prom. Both are painful and may have lasting effects, but the former has a dimension of terror to it. The other causes sleepless nights and maybe an aching heart, but a date can still be a fun time. The football player got over his fear of public speaking; the woman attacked in the parking lot of the shopping mall lives with the terror for the rest of her life.

3. *Fear can be helpful.* Although fear is uncomfortable, sometimes terrifying, it has its positive side. It makes sense to be afraid of HIV, AIDS, cancer, heart disease, violent people, poisonous snakes, driving an automobile on icy highways, and anything that can hurt us and others. We teach children not to talk to strangers or accept candy or rides from people they do not know. While walking in the neighborhood, I have to be cautious in how I greet people. I can no longer stop to talk to the children. Children are taught to be afraid of strangers—people. This is a great loss to them and to us, yet it is necessary in our world.

Fear is a basic emotion, part of our native equipment. As with all normal emotions, fear has a positive function to perform. Comforting formulas for getting rid of anxiety may be just the wrong thing. Books about "peace of mind" can be bad medicine. To be afraid when one should be afraid is good sense.[1]

4. *We respond to fear in different ways.* Some people freeze when afraid. They become victims of their fear or the source of their

fear. Spouse-abuse victims often are captives of their abusive spouses (97 percent of whom are men). Although afraid of the next battering, the slap, the slamming against the wall, and the big fist plunging into the stomach, the abused is even more afraid to leave because the abuser has warned her that he will kill her if she leaves him or if she tells anyone about the beatings. He threatens to track her down and stab her, shoot her, or beat her to death. Often, the victim is also an economic prisoner; she does not have the resources to support herself and her children. She certainly will not leave the children with the violent man. Although there is help through agencies for victims of abuse, they are often afraid to seek that help. People with phobias are also prisoners of their illnesses, their fears. Edward Burke captures this process when he writes, "No passion so effectively robs the mind of all its powers of acting and reasoning as fear."[2] That does not have to be the case; we do not have to be the victim of some of our fears.

Some people confront their fears. William Burham believes, "The most drastic and usually the most effective remedy for fear is direct action."[3] Susan Jeffers agrees. She writes:

> Pushing through fear is less frightening than living with the underlying fear that comes from a feeling of helplessness...I know it's hard to take at first. It says that no matter how "secure" any of us feel in the little cocoon we have built for ourselves, we live, consciously or unconsciously, with the fear that the day of reckoning will eventually come.[4]

This can be a very difficult task; it is much easier to write than to do.

The first step in confronting the fear is to admit it. Tell someone how you feel; maybe describe the anguish you feel and the sleepless nights of tossing and tumbling and late-night television, with all those bulky people telling you how to get in shape with their new exercise machines.

- Some people need a therapist to help them deal with their phobias.
- Other people need a friend to talk to about their fears of elevators or intimacy.

- Some need a group of people to help them confront their fear of dying or depression.
- Some people need all the above—and a whole lot of prayer.

When the fear seems irrational, it is difficult to admit it to others. For example, we "feel silly" to be afraid of elevators especially since, statistically, we are less likely to be hurt in an elevator than in an automobile accident. Or we may be afraid that others will find out that we are afraid of germs.

Second, after admitting our fear, identifying and describing the source of the fear sometimes helps to relieve the agonizing pain. The fear of water is something we learn. Usually, the fear is the result of a terrifying experience, such as swallowing a mouthful of water when we were learning to swim or being abandoned by our mother or father while in the water. Not too many years ago, it was common for parents to throw their children into a lake, river, pool, or pond and say, "Sink or swim." Of course, the parent believed the child could swim before the toss, but the child did not know it and often panicked, resulting in a lifelong fear of water. Being tossed in the water and abandoned (forced to swim for our lives) may damage our trust in our parents and other people.

Although identifying and describing fear may give some relief, it will not make the pain go away. Telling someone we are afraid of water will not automatically abolish the fear of swimming.

Dorothy Thompson captured the process when she wrote, "There is nothing to fear except the persistent refusal to try to find out the truth, the persistent refusal to analyze the causes of happenings. Fear grows in darkness. If you think there's a bogeyman around, turn on the light."[5] Thompson is a little cold with her advice to those who suffer from paralyzing fear, but she is correct in theory.

5. *We have to take action to get relief from feelings of fear.* In *The Gift of Fear,* Gavin de Becker describes his early experiences of violence.

A woman was pointing a gun at her husband who was standing with his hands held out in front of him. She was anxiously changing her grip on the small semi-automatic pistol.

"Now I'm going to kill you," she repeated quietly, almost as if to herself. I was startled, but not surprised. The silence that followed, however, did concern me.

My plan had been to take the child out of the house. But I abandoned that and told her to stay in the bed. At two years old, she probably didn't understand the seriousness of the situation, but I was ten and knew all about these things.

It wasn't the first time I'd heard that gun go off in the house: my mother had accidentally fired it toward me a few months earlier, the bullet passing so close to my ear that I felt it buzz in the air before striking the wall. On the way back to our living room, I stopped when I smelled the gunpowder. I listened, trying to figure out what was happening without looking into the room. It was too quiet.[6]

De Becker's mother had shot her husband
De Becker lived in this violent household with his mother, sister, and stepfathers. His early years were filled with violence. His response was to become an expert in predicting when violence would occur. *The Gift of Fear* describes ways that we may predict violence. His clients are a "wide-ranging group: federal government agencies (including the U. S. Marshals Service, the Federal Reserve Board, and the Central Intelligence Agency), prosecutors, giant corporations, universities, television stars,"[7] and the list goes on and on. His agency is in demand because he knows the signs of violence and can help us to diminish our risk of becoming a victim. He helps people reduce their suffering from fear by teaching them how to avoid violence when possible. Instead of becoming a criminal, as is the case for many people who grow up in such an environment, de Becker uses his fear to help others.

We may be able to use our fear to help others and diminish the suffering that surrounds us. When we overcome our fear by using it to defeat the demons that haunt us, it becomes something positive and powerful. MADD, hospice, the Helping

Hands program for patients with Alzheimer's Disease, Alcoholics Anonymous, and other support and action groups reach out to make a difference to those suffering. These helpers know that they are making a difference in the lives of others by the ways that they respond to suffering.

Responses to Suffering:
Prayer

Chapter 6

Pray!

While Catherine and I were speaking at a Christian Women's Fellowship retreat at a Kentucky state park, a woman gave me the following note.

A sign in a beauty parlor reads:
So far today, God, I've done all right. I haven't gossiped, haven't lost my temper, haven't been grumpy, selfish, or overindulgent. I'm really glad about that. But in a few minutes, God, I'm going to get out of bed, and from then on I'm probably going to need a lot of help. Thank you. In Jesus' name, Amen.

We pray because we need a lot of help either in solving our own or others' suffering, and we need a lot of help in celebrating the great moments of love and joy that enrich our lives. We need a lot of help from God, from others, and from God through others.

People responding to the question "What do people do or say that is helpful to those suffering?" often suggested that people pray for themselves and for others. After reading their suggestions, I wanted to learn more about how people prayed. I developed the following questionnaire. Take time to respond to the questions before reading what others said and then compare your prayer practices and expectations to those of others.

1. Do you pray daily? If so, how many times do you pray? Please describe.
2. Do you pray for the same people and situations every day?
3. Do you have a special place and time for praying? Please describe.
4. Do you believe that God is listening every time you pray?
5. Does prayer affect the way you feel
   5.1. about yourself?
   5.2. about others?
   5.3. about God?
6. Does prayer change anything
   6.1. in our work?
   6.2. in interpersonal relationships (family, friends, enemies, etc)?
   6.3. in health? Does prayer heal? If so, how does this happen?
   6.4. in the world?
   6.5. in ourselves?
7. What are the benefits of praying? Please describe.

There was great variety in the expectations and practices of those responding to the questionnaire. There are those who pray several times a day and interject special prayers when a crisis arises. There are those who pray occasionally, maybe a couple of times a week. Some people pray only when they or someone they care about is suffering in some way. Others pray for the same people every day. James Brewer-Calvert wrote the following description of the benefits of praying:

> Prayer benefits my life at every level. Physically, it slows my pulse and lowers my blood pressure. It lifts my resistance to stress and probably over time even increases my immunity to disease. Emotionally, I can face challenges with greater calm and resolve. Pausing to pray helps me to think things through more clearly. I am less likely to aggravate my life situation by acting in negative, hurtful ways. I can nurture better attitudes and greater caring as I sincerely pray for those in need, including those I may consider less than friendly. But the greatest benefit is spiritual. Prayer opens me to the

presence, love, and guidance of God. Prayer nurtures
my spirit and awakens the truth within me that I am
more than flesh, blood, and animalistic drives. Prayer
not only reminds me I am a child of God, but nourishes
that child within me.[1]

This is a moving description of the benefits of praying. However,
I would disagree on one point. All of the above are spiritual.
We cannot separate the spiritual from the other dimensions of
life. I think James would agree that all living is a spiritual
challenge.

My friend Mel helped me to understand this concept.
Several years ago he confessed how angry he was at an
acquaintance. The man spread rumors that Mel was
incompetent, negligent in his job, bordered on being unethical–
and, in fact, that Mel was an immoral person. We can
understand why Mel was angry. If certain people believed this
information, Mel would lose his reputation as a man of integrity,
and he could lose his job. I was caught up in his emotion and
the unjust actions of the rumormonger.

"You have to confront him, and you have do it as soon as
possible," I ordered.

"No, Loren, I can't do that now. I have a lot of praying to
do before I can confront him. I am too angry." He prayed for
his enemy and for himself.

Mel did not ask God to fix it, to solve his problem without
involving him in the solution. Mel asked God to fix it by
involving him in the process, by changing him. And eventually
God did. That was a miracle! Turning hostility into
understanding and peace within oneself–that is the power of
prayer affecting how we feel about ourselves, others, and God.
Prayer changed the way Mel dealt with his relationship with
an enemy, and his praying helped to heal him and the
relationship.

Intercessory prayer is praying for someone else, hoping
that our prayers will help the person in some way. It is talking
to God about someone for whom we are concerned. Religious
people try to help by praying for one another and for others
who may not be religious in the same way that they are.

Most people appreciate others' praying for them. So when we pray for people it is often helpful to tell them that we are praying for them. This assures them that we care and are trying to be a part of their lives in a significant way. We take time to think about and feel for, and with, them.

Some people believe that the more people who pray for a particular person or for a particular problem to be solved, the more likely the prayer is to be answered in the way that the people praying want. There is much disagreement about this belief, and sometimes this concept leads to disappointment.

The optical nerve in Catherine's left eye was shriveling up and dying. Because she was active with the International Christian Women's Fellowship, word spread rapidly that she was about to lose the sight in her eye. A few months later, an acquaintance approached her at a church meeting. Easing up to Catherine, Irene, in a quiet, confidential tone meant to communicate concern, said, "Our church circle has been praying for you ever since we learned about your illness. How is your eye?"

"I lost the sight in it a few months ago."

Irene's mouth dropped open. Her eyes appeared almost dazed. She was shocked that their prayers had not persuaded God to heal Catherine. God was supposed to answer *their* prayers. After all, the prayers were for someone else. They expressed the compassion God wants from us. She was not only disappointed, she was dejected—her church circle failed or God failed—something went wrong.

Prayer is not talking a reluctant God into granting us our wish. It is much more than that and cannot be tested on the saving of the sight in an eye or other types of suffering.

Pray for others; tell them you are praying for them; and even if the specifics of your prayers are not answered in the way you want, be a friend to the person for whom you are praying. That just might do more good in the long run than what you thought the person needed most.

A Roman Catholic sister was struggling with her faith and went to Father Thomas H. Green seeking help. Green writes:

The uncertainties of the time forced her to confront the abyss of faith. She was a beautifully honest person, very direct and sincere. Thus I was nonplussed when she said to me one day: "Let me ask you just one question: Is God really real for you?" After hesitating a long moment, I said, "Yes. I'm sure he is. But I don't know how I can prove it to you." Her answer surprised and humbled me. "No, that's not necessary," she said. "As long as I know that he is real to you, that is reason enough for me to keep searching."[2]

The people responding to the questionnaire said in many different ways: Pray for you, pray for me, too, and pray for those who have trouble praying for themselves.

Chapter 7

Our Prayers Reveal Who We Are

We tend to think of prayer as a form of magic to get what we want. New Testament scholar Sharyn Dowd explains how this has been a problem for centuries:

> Ancient writers were correct when they distinguished magic from religion by arguing that whereas a magician harnesses divine power to do his own will, the religious person prays for divine power in order to do the will of the deity, or submits to the will of the gods in the absence of their intervention on his or her belief.[1]

This confusion causes some shallow requests from, and almost obscene credit to, God. It turns God into an amazon.com shopping Web site. I can just see God sitting at the divine computer reacting to the Internet request and credits.

"Loren wants a better golf swing. He ought to know better than that. You want a better golf swing, see a pro and practice."

"Sara wants me to help her win the beauty contest."

"John just gave me credit for his victory over that pulverized, pathetic boxer. That sure hurts my reputation."

"Oh no! That rock star just thanked me for choosing him over the other rock stars to win the Grammy award."

Our prayers reveal who we are and what we value.

I am confused and amused by a prayer by Lancelot Andrewes, a bishop in the Church of England in the sixteenth century: "Thou didst look upon Magdalene at the feast, Peter in the hall, the thief on the wood." The bishop was hard on himself, describing himself as "an unclean worm, a dead dog, a putrid corpse," but at the same time as "the work of thine hands."[2]

There is something both pathetic and amusing in that prayer. Andrewes insults God by giving God credit for creating an unclean worm, a dead dog, and a putrid corpse. The bad-boy bishop had a limited understanding of God.

Jimmy Breslin won the Pulitzer Prize for Distinguished Commentary in 1986. Breslin was the author of several books and a man much admired for his insights into life and his ability to describe human events. Breslin describes his thoughts while being rolled in for brain surgery, when one of his fears was that he would come out of surgery unable to remember verbs: "I knew that if something happened to the curl in my brain that causes verbs, I would be one of those home relief cases that people hate so much."[3]

He describes the visit from the priest just before he went into surgery.

> The priest suggested that we say a prayer. So my daughter, wife, and I and the priest held hands in a circle and he said the Our Father and I don't know what other prayer was recited, if any. I concentrated on my Act of Contrition again. But we were in this tight circle, a huddle, and I thought of these college teams in a huddle praying to God before they ran out onto the field. What the hell is that all about? Praying for a first down? What kind of value is that? Young primitives with their eyes closed, not even knowing the words of a prayer, they hardly know their name; grasping coaches asking God to get them a Nike contract.[4]

Breslin said to his wife and daughter, "Don't worry, I'm in the state of Grace if I go...I meant it as a half smart remark and also as a statement of fact." That is who Breslin was.

Our prayers reveal who we are. We pray for a mother who is battling cancer, a friend who is depressed after being fired from a job he held for twenty years, or a child who was abandoned by her single parent. We need a large dose of hope to hang in there and do what we can to relieve the suffering of someone we care about. That is who we are.

Our prayers reveal those times when we are overwhelmed with gratitude for a caring friend, an adolescent who has overcome an addiction to drugs, a sunny day, a walk on the beach on a rainy day holding hands with our senior citizen spouse who makes our day and our life. We need to store those special moments in our memory banks to carry us through the tough times. That is who we are.

We read about the terrorizing and killing of citizens in Kosovo, and we want to weep, but instead we say a prayer for the people who have been taught to hate those who are not like them. Then we ask for forgiveness for our prejudice born of an unforgiving culture. We pray that we will not hurt others who are not like us. Then we remember the words of Dietrich Bonhoeffer, "We cannot condemn or hate those for whom we pray."[5]

Bonhoeffer's life and writings give us a guide for meeting life's tragedies and joys. Bonhoeffer was a pastor, preacher, and professor in Germany during World War II. He refused to endorse the Nazi political policies that led to the Holocaust, the ruthless killing of Jews and others who opposed Hitler. He spoke out in opposition to Hitler, denouncing a "political system that corrupted and grossly misled a nation and made the 'Führer' its idol and god."[6] He also joined a resistance movement to assassinate Hitler. The Nazis arrested him.

In prison Bonhoeffer continued his practice of getting up every day at 6:00 a.m. to have a talk with God. He wrote, "We are silent at the beginning of the day because God should have the first word, and we are silent before going to sleep because the last word belongs to God."[7] While conducting a worship service for other prisoners, two Nazi guards came to escort him on the brief trail that led to the gallows. He knew he was going to die. As he was led to his execution, Bonhoeffer said to the other prisoners, "This is the end, for me the beginning of life."[8] That is who Bonhoeffer was.

Conditions affect the results of prayer, and especially the one praying. Staying in touch with God daily prepares us for both the joys of life, those special gifts of grace, and for those tragedies that tear at our hearts and bodies. Thomas Merton, the renowned Roman Catholic monk and mystic, once suggested, "Most people do not experience God's presence in a sudden flash, but by gradual, almost imperceptible steps."[9]

Larry Dossey claims, "In scores of scientific experiments dealing with prayer and prayer-like states of consciousness, one of the most crucial qualities appears to be love-compassion, empathy, and deep caring."[10] We do not need scientific proof to believe that compassion affects what happens when people pray for one another. I am not one to try and prove prayer, but it makes sense to believe that those who pray out of a feeling of compassion are most likely to do something about that for which they pray. I do not understand how prayer works, but I certainly believe that prayer works in mysterious and mystical ways.

When my brother Andy was two years old, our mother told me that she had to live until Andy was twelve years old. She had been diagnosed with tuberculosis. That was in 1946. At that time tuberculosis was thought to be a death signal. The physician let her stay home, teaching her and our father how to prevent spreading the disease to him and us. Two years later we were out of money and deeply in debt. Our father told the physician about our financial situation and that we had borrowed all we could. My father assured the physician that he would pay him as he could. The doctor replied, "I don't carry charity cases," and ordered my mother to the state sanatorium in Orlando, Florida. We lived miles away in Jacksonville, Florida.

The separation from her baby, Andy, was more painful than the disease. Three years later, she was released from the sanatorium because she had cancer. During the next five years she became increasingly worse with operation following operation. One physician told me that he did not understand how my mother was alive. She became a case study for other physicians. Finally, she was released from the hospital to die at home. The last six months were tormented ones for my father and younger brothers Ted and Andy, who lived at home. The physician instructed my father to give my mother morphine shots every four hours. After two hours my mother would beg for relief from the excruciating pain. The crying and begging carried with it an excruciating price in suffering for both my mother and father. With her dying and in such pain, I never understood why the doctors were concerned about her becoming addicted to morphine.

On Andy's twelfth birthday, our mother died. I do not understand the phenomenon that took place with my mother. Some people would say she willed herself to stay alive in spite of the pain and physiological factors. Others would claim her body, mind, and spirit worked together to meet her commitment to Andy. Still others would say that prayer made God intervene to grant my mother's wish. If that is so, why didn't God intervene to eliminate my parents' suffering? Why does God not intervene for others who pray to live or for those who pray to die to escape tormenting pain?

"Pray without ceasing" is the biblical advice given by Paul (1 Thessalonians 5:17). This suggests that prayer is more than saying words and making requests of God. Prayer presupposes an attitude that sets the environment for inviting God into our lives. We need to find our own way of staying in touch with God, for that is who we are.

Prayer is not

- only saying words; prayer is also listening.
- just thinking; prayer is also feeling.
- merely asking; prayer is also giving.
- simply doing; prayer is also being.

Prayer is

- a way of life.
- an attitude toward God, others, and ourselves.
- a way of responding to suffering.

I do not understand many of these things, but I believe that God answers prayer, if not in one way, then in another. God is always present with us, in times of suffering and in times of rejoicing. Listening for that presence and noticing God in our midst during our daily routines of living prepares us for anything that life throws at us. If we know that God is with us in our suffering, we have hope. We believe that love will overcome hate, that action will overcome apathy, and that life will overcome death, *eventually*.

Chapter 8

Finding God in Prayer

Comedian Flip Wilson once said, "I'm getting ready to pray; anyone want anything?" We pray because we want something for ourselves or someone else. In fact, we are motivated to act by our wants and needs.

"God, fix it, but don't bother me in the process."

"God, my cholesterol is over 400. Fix it; in the meantime I will be at Cracker Barrel eating their Country Sampler breakfast: country ham, smoked sausage and bacon, red eye gravy, smoked house gravy, eggs, biscuits, and lots of coffee with that rich cream. Fix my cholesterol, God."

"God, as you know, I have maxed out my six credit cards, and the creditors are closing in on me. This is an emergency. I will cut up my Discover card and only use my Visa until you get this cleared up."

"God, my spouse and I are in real trouble. He criticizes me all the time; I can't seem to do anything to please him. Fix it God; change him into a nice, sensitive, caring person who will get off my back."

"God, I've been through a lot preparing for this wedding. My life has been filled with sleepless nights and long hours of making out a guest list, buying a wedding gown, trying to satisfy my mother and future mother-in-law, kissing George with the feeling of a mummy, selecting the color of icing for the cake, and taking care of a thousand other details that go along with a large wedding. I am exhausted and look like it. God, I'm calling on you for a makeover for my face, emotions, and mind. Incidentally, the wedding is tomorrow."

"God, fix it! My spouse is suffering from Alzheimer's disease, and I don't know what to do. I am so tired and confused."

That is the normal response to tragedy. We call on God to do that which we cannot–fix the loved one who is fast falling into oblivion. We want a fast solution to the problem of suffering–for them and us. "God, eliminate the tragedy; don't bother me with the details." The amazing thing is that sometimes God seems to do just that. Often God answers our prayers through a skilled surgeon, an empathetic pastor, a faithful friend, a loving parent or child, or a forgiving spirit.

There are other times when we pray for our loved one to be relieved of suffering. We are willing to endure almost anything if we can believe that the loved one will be spared a tormented future. We need a large dose of hope to "hang in there" and do what we can to relieve the suffering of someone we care about. So we pray for Sara or Sam and for ourselves, sometimes in the face of great odds. God, fix it.

We were expecting my brother and sister-in-law from Florida to come for a visit in September. Catherine called the people who clean our house and scheduled them to clean before the company was to arrive, but the women did not show up. So I asked Catherine how much she paid the women to clean the house. "Fifty dollars," she replied.

I reflected and said, "There is a book at Joseph Beth Bookstore I've wanted for two years. I haven't been able to bring myself to spend sixty dollars on the book. It's about the paintings in the Louvre." Catherine looked at me with a faint smile on her face and said, "I'll pay you fifty dollars to clean the house." I thought about how I don't like to clean the house, especially dusting. I thought about the book and said, "Okay." It was almost a pleasure cleaning the house.

We may be motivated to do something because we need or want something else, and that sometimes changes our *attitude* toward that for which we pray. Listen to this biblical narrative about a widow who persistently asked the judge for justice (Luke 18:1–8).

In Jesus' day, the judge in many cases had total control of court decisions. If you went before a judge for a crime or litigation of some kind, your case was presented, and the judge decided. It was over; you either lost or won the case. The word *widow* was used in parables to represent those who needed to be defended but did not have the money to hire a lawyer or, in some cases, even to get their grievance heard before a judge. They did not have the power to buy justice. In those days, the more money and political power one had, the more justice one got.

So the widow went to the judge every day to plead her case. The judge did not care for the widow or what she wanted, nor did he fear any kind of divine judgment for his actions. The judge was an emotionally cold man. The widow badgered him, she irritated him, and she nagged him. Finally, the judge, exasperated, gave in and granted the woman what she wanted just to get rid of her. The parable assures us, "Will not God grant justice to his chosen ones who cry to him day and night? Will he delay long in helping them? I tell you, he will quickly grant justice to them" (Luke 18:7–8).

The point of the parable is that persistence in prayer pays off. We should pray daily and often, so the scriptures tell us. The story also tells us that our prayers may not be answered right away, but we should not lose heart. We may have to practice patience when praying, which is very difficult for many of us.

The spiritual writers of the past were often people living in monasteries who cherished the solitude of a stroll in the woods, a visit to the lake just to watch the seagulls land on the water, or a chance to see the sun rise over the rolling waves of the ocean. No fast fishing or competitive swimming or boat races for these people. They were at home with the slow pace of meditation, contemplation, and simple prayer. They were our teachers of prayer; they wrote the prayer books and gave the lectures on spirituality. What about those of us who are wired differently, whose minds enjoy playing with ideas at a fast pace? What about those of us who cannot seem to stop our minds long enough to meditate for fifteen minutes, who have trouble waiting on God's answer? We think in seconds; God thinks in centuries.

Recently, I read *Driven to Distraction*,[1] a book about Attention Deficit Disorder (ADD), a malfunctioning of the brain.

Both authors are psychiatrists, and both have ADD. The ten million people who have ADD have fast-moving minds; their minds are almost always channel surfing. It is very difficult for them to stay focused. To tell them to meditate or to pray for thirty minutes and then sit and listen for God's answer would be unrealistic. Their minds do not work that way.

How about those of us who are Type-A personalities and enjoy the fast pace? Rising at 4:30 a.m. to spend an hour in prayer does not work for me. I don't even know who I am at 4:30 a.m. That form of spiritual discipline only leads to frustration for one who channel surfs with a five-second pause between each television channel. After the first few minutes of meditation and prayer, my mind begins to review the day's to-do list, to plan an approach to the current problem, and to select a place to have lunch.

What do we do for people who are not programmed for the Middle Ages method of meditation? Jesus said to go into the closet to pray, which simply means that we should take time to pray without making a show of it for other people.

What about prayer in a different mode? There is not just one way or a best way to pray, meditate, or contemplate. We each need to find our own way of staying in touch with God, to pray at our own pace. Finding God in prayer is a personal matter. It challenges us to find our own way of noticing and responding to God in our daily lives.

Let's look at a few of the ways that people pray and the closets in which they pray.

One person very close to me discovered that the only privacy she had when three sons lived at home was in the bathtub; so her prayer time was in the tub. She also has a very personal conversation with God during Holy Communion in her worship service. Another person told me that his main prayer time is in the hot tub. The following are some of the "prayer closets" people attending a session on prayer listed: in bed; while cleaning the house, gardening, cooking, or jogging; at the breakfast table; and at the dining room table before the children get up. I use my daily hour of walking as my main prayer time.

Other people begin the day with a short prayer for guidance and protection for their children, spouse, other family members, and people with special needs. They close the day with a prayer of thanksgiving. My friend Dr. William O. Paulsell begins the day by reading a psalm, meditating, having intercessory prayer, and contemplating. It is an hour of renewal for him. I have tried his method. Have you ever really read the Psalms? Norman Vincent Peale, the author of *The Power of Positive Thinking,*[2] did not write them. The Psalms deal with reality in an uncompromising way. After a few weeks of reading the Psalms, I started the day exhausted, a little depressed, and defensive. That method of staying in touch with God works for Paulsell and many others; it does not help me stay in touch with God.

We have to find our particular way of praying. We need to keep in mind that the purpose of prayer is to keep us in touch with God and ourselves. The method is not the primary issue. God is waiting for us to realize that God's presence patiently seeks our attention. Persistence in prayer reminds us of that presence.

Persistent praying teaches us about

- the nature of God's love,
- the sacredness of life,
- the value of each person,
- the beauty of relationships,
- the support of friends, and
- the loyalty of family.

We need this vision to help us cope with suffering. Persistence in prayer pays because it reminds us who and what is important. Even when our prayers are not answered in the way that we want, we may feel the presence of God through the people who love us.

Marjorie Suchocki is a process theologian who believes that God is in the world acting and reacting with us to create the world as it should be. In such a world, God hurts and rejoices with us in a loving way.[3]

Suchocki writes not from the perspective of one who sits behind a mahogany desk with a Microsoft word processor using words to describe theories about suffering and prayer, but from the perspective of one who sits in a hospital waiting for the verdict of the physician after an operation, and who listens to the words of the minister describe her son-in-law at graveside. She feels and speaks of the importance of the hug of a mother and the comforting lap of a grandmother at such times. Her son-in-law died at thirty-eight years of age, leaving three young children and her daughter. Suchocki lived through the agony of watching her mother die from cancer. She knows how it is to plead with God to heal her mother, only to feel as Jesus felt when he said, "My God, my God, why have you forsaken me?" Listen to her powerful words of pain: "God, you are healing this stupid sore, but it's not her sore that's the problem, it's her liver; why can't you do something?"[4]

When her mother was dying in the hospital room, Suchocki and her brothers stood around the bed, each touching their mother. Suchocki wrote:

> We were touching the profound places of the human spirit in that hospital room, and discovering that the process of dying was holy. Then she looked up at us all, and said, "My heart is filled with overwhelming love." I knew then that my prayers were answered, and my mother died a healthy woman. There is no health that is deeper than death.[5]

She explains that after the death of her son-in-law,

> We continued in our prayers. On my visits to Dallas, my growing grandchildren would throw themselves in my arms, covering me with hugs and kisses, and I would know that they were healing: a child who can still love openly, having suffered great loss, is a healthy child.[6]

It is this grandmother, mother, and mother-in-law who reasons: "In an interdependent, relational, contextual world, our praying constitutes a dance with God that makes a difference to what God can do in the world. For God works with the world as it is to lead it to what it can be."[7]

Suchocki found God in suffering and in hugs and kisses. Her prayers were answered in some ways that did not fit her wants or expectations. Her prayers were answered by the presence that makes a difference in us, between God and us, and between others and us. Her prayers made a difference in

God as well as God making a difference in her. Both suffered a great loss and grieved together.

There are those who think that we should not pray for ourselves or for what we want, but just pray that we may do the will of God. Selfish prayers, they contend, are beneath God and are a form of self-indulgence. That is not only unrealistic; it is a distorted sense of God's relationship with God's creation.

If you are in pain, hurting or suffering in any way, God wants to hear about it. God wants us to know that God is suffering with us. Our concern is not with the methods of prayer or "closets of prayer"; our deepest need is to stay in touch with God in times of suffering and in times of joy and celebration.

Responses to Suffering: Listening, Thinking, and Talking

Chapter 9

The Variety of Ways of Responding

In *Dakota: A Spiritual Journal,* Kathleen Norris tells how two women responded to their suffering with cancer.

"If I ever get out of this hospital, I'm going to look out for number one," said one woman. And that's exactly what she did. Against overwhelming odds, she survived, and it made her mean. The other woman spoke about the blessings of a life that had taken some hard blows. Her mother had killed herself when she was a girl and her husband had died young. I happened to visit her just after she'd been told that she had less than a year to live. She was dry-eyed, and had been reading the Psalms. She was entirely realistic about her illness and said to me, "The one thing that scares me is the pain. I hope I die before I turn into an old bitch." I told her family that story after the funeral, and they loved it; they could hear in it their mother's voice, the way she really was.[1]

How do we respond when we are suffering? We will examine the ways specific people deal with and talk about pain, loss, and sorrow. Some seem to thrive on their suffering. Others become bitter. Some people respond creatively to their problems. Some saints and sinners pray. There are those who cry and those who curse family members, God, and themselves. Imaginative people come out of their suffering smiling, while others turn on their families and friends. Some people blame

God; others blame themselves for their suffering. Some people return to the church, while others leave the church for failing to do all it could. Some people are grateful for the time that they have to live. Others condemn God for prolonging their pain. Some people curse the pain; others plead for a few minutes of relief. Some people scream, while others laugh. Some of us fight the suffering; others yield to it. One person responds with joy, another with bitterness that could cut through granite. What do we say to these people?

Simone Weil thanked God for caring enough to send the best God had to offer in suffering. Was this a normal response to suffering? Was she a masochistic, manic-depressive person or a saint? What is normal? We will examine some of the issues these questions raise and other problems and challenges created by suffering. What do we say to people like Ms. Weil?

Sara is a faithful member of the church to which she belongs. She enjoys visiting friends and acquaintances when they are in the hospital. It is a good day for Sara when she can "skip" from room to room bringing a little joy to the sick. That is how she perceives herself. She charges into a hospital room and takes over with her tense body and almost rap words. One day, Sara burst into Mary's room, rushed past me, stood by the side of the hospital bed, and asked Mary how she was doing.

"I'm doing all right," Mary said.

"What do you have? Why are you in the hospital?" asked Sara.

"Dr. Jones said that I need my gallbladder removed. He said there is nothing to worry about, that I will probably be home in less than a week."

"I wouldn't be too sure about that," replied Sara. "Jean had the same operation last year and died."

Responding in a helpful way to the suffering of others is a major problem for many people. What do we say? What do we do? What do we think? How should we feel? Those are some of the questions that arise when we have to relate to Debra in depression, John with cancer, and Betty in a divorce battle. What do we do and say?

Why do some people get angry with us when we try to help them? "Why would the gift of a cake offend Joan?" asked Melanie.

"What in the world has gotten into John to cause him to treat me like a stray dog? A heart attack is not an excuse to talk to people like that. Why would my saying, 'It was God's will' upset John?"

"Why did George get angry when I told him that if he prayed more, God would help cure him?" "Why does Ralph resent even a hint that he might be hurting when he broke his leg?" "Why does Ann cry at the slightest suggestion that she could get hurt in the relationship?"

Is there a difference between pain and suffering? If so, does the person hurting care? As their three children slept during the ride back from a July fireworks show, the parents stopped at a park for a bathroom break. When they came out of the restroom, the van was gone. It had rolled into the Columbia River, and the children drowned. When the children's grandfather heard about the accident, he said, "It's a tragedy. I tell myself these things happen, I suppose, even if it's hard to understand why. The Lord knows what he's doing." The grandfather implies through his statement that somehow God had a hand in the deaths of the three children. Is God involved in such tragedies? Many people think so. Believing God is involved with suffering somehow gives some people hope and a small measure of relief from their grief.

What part does one's faith play in responding to suffering? Does it make a difference what we believe about God's involvement in suffering? If so, how does it make a difference to you and me, and what does that difference mean for us now and in the future? Whether we want to or not, sooner or later we will have to deal with how God is involved in suffering.

While attending an ecumenical Thanksgiving worship service at Bethsaida Baptist Church in Lexington, Kentucky, I heard a choir sing several hymns and songs quite beautifully. But one hymn stayed with me, not only because of the tune but because of the refrain. The choir would sing a verse, and then with joy and excitement, the voices would ring out, "He may not come when I want him, but he'll be on time." It may seem that God is not with us when we want God to fix our suffering. Maybe God is present, and we do not see or feel God because God is not giving us what we want at that time. Does that mean God is not present?

When my son Philip told Jerry Small, a mutual friend, that I was researching and writing a book on suffering, Jerry told the following story.

A family in a small town in Wisconsin was living a happy life. Then something happened that changed them forever. Angie, seven years old, died from spinal meningitis. It was extremely painful for everyone. The mother and father grieved and were confused. They kept asking why God let such a terrible thing happen to such an innocent little girl. After the funeral, there was a radical change in Eric, Angie's four-year-old brother. Instead of being a carefree boy who enjoyed playing with friends and usually doing what his parents wanted him to, Eric fussed with his friends and argued with his parents about everything. He was a problem for his parents. For four years different therapists worked with Eric without success. He continued to be antisocial, hostile, and rude to everyone. Nothing helped Eric until someone discovered that Eric had heard an aunt say at Angie's funeral, "Only the good die young." Eric was being "bad" to keep from dying.

It matters what we say and do in the company of people who are suffering. Innocent bystanders may get hurt.

Chapter 10

Blaming the Victim

At the World Day of Prayer in Kaneohe, Hawaii, in May 1993, Korean researcher Yun Chung-ok spoke on the subject of "comfort women" during World War II in Korea. Japanese officers selected girls twelve years of age and older, including young adults, for the sexual "comfort" of the soldiers. They claimed it was a morale booster for the soldiers. The young women were placed in cubicles. The soldiers lined up outside, and one by one entered the cubicles and raped the young women. This continued until the victims were either dead or near dead. To further humiliate and dehumanize these innocent victims of atrocious abuse, the women were given new names so that they could be called these names while being raped.

These acts not only damaged the women's bodies, it crushed their sense of worth as women in an Asian culture. The women thought of themselves, as did others, as "damaged property." The women felt guilty for what had happened to them. After the war and even to this day, some of these women still suffer total rejection from others—no respect, no spouse, no family, and a life not worth living.

Researcher Yun Chung-ok and others are trying to change these attitudes and practices. Unfortunately, the raping of women during war is not uncommon throughout the world. On March 28, 1993, an Associated Press release read, "Activists asked yesterday that the United Nations do more to protect women in war-torn Yugoslavia from being raped and killed." In December 1999, an article reported the same crimes as being committed in Bosnia. Every year since I began writing this book, there have been reports of the raping of women in war-torn countries.

It is not uncommon for victims of abuse to be blamed for the crime. One response to suffering is to blame the one who is suffering. Catherine and I agreed to be the resource leaders for a regional ministers and spouses retreat at Estes Park, Colorado. During the year preceding the retreat we corresponded with Arthur, the minister who was organizing the event. When we arrived at the park, Raymond, a minister in the region, greeted us and said that he had to discuss an important issue immediately. As we ate lunch, he told us about a series of events that had taken place with Arthur.

A woman in his congregation had accused Arthur of seducing her. When she went public with the sexual affair, six other women came forward to accuse Arthur of having sex with them. All these women had gone to Arthur for counseling. These women were lonely and needed help coping with the emotional needs that came with being mothers, spouses, lovers, and professional persons.

When the affairs became public, scores of people blamed the women for seducing the minister. They were called names usually given to people who make a living selling sex. Arthur was married and had three children, ranging in age from ten to sixteen. As the whole community knew about this church crisis, it was embarrassing and painful for all the families and friends involved. The outrageous aspect of this drama is that the congregation voted to keep Arthur as their minister and to discount the testimony of those who had been abused. Many in the community continually ostracized the women. The women were the victims in this case because the minister used their emotional vulnerability to satisfy his sexual desires. Blame the victim!

This incident not only damaged these women's belief in Arthur a minister who cared about them as persons, but it damaged their belief in the church, in a God who cares about them, and in a community dedicated to meeting the spiritual and emotional needs of people. These women violated one of the unwritten and unspoken rules of some local church congregations: Do not tell the truth about what is going on in our little community. John Irving puts it this way: "The code of small towns is simple but encompassing: if many forms of craziness are allowed, many forms of cruelty are ignored."[1]

In her excellent book *Trauma and Recovery,* Judith Lewis Herman stresses this point when she writes, "The church often creates a community of secrets—that is, do not confess what horrible things happened to you—or what you think or feel (incest, child abuse, adultery, etc.)."[2] When someone embarrasses the members of such a church, they often turn on the victim.

In the church and society the victim often gets blamed for his or her suffering. In a rape trial, the judge dismisses the case because the woman was "asking for it." At the time of the rape, the woman was wearing a short skirt, tight-fitting sweater, and shoes with stiletto heels. This happened several years ago in a small town. It still takes place in a more disguised way today if the rapist gets a clever attorney. The victim becomes the criminal and is humiliated for letting the man rape her.

"Believe me when I tell you I am sick," Carol urged those who questioned her sickness. People were accusing her of pretending to be sick to get special treatment. This is not unusual. When the child says, "I am sick and can't go to school today," the parent may ask, "Are you sick, or do you just not want to go to school?" The implication is that the child is faking sickness to avoid something unpleasant at school. We blame the child for "being sick." Whether the child is faking a stomachache or not, the desire to avoid school tells us that the child is hurting in some way.

There is a biblical concept that proclaims the same idea. Jesus healed the lame man saying, "Stand up, take your mat and walk." Later, Jesus found a former invalid in the temple and said to him, "See, you have been made well! Do not sin any more, so that nothing worse happens to you" (John 5:8, 14). It was the man's fault that he was lame; he had sinned and had been punished with a physical impairment for sinning. Whether we think sin causes sickness is not the point here. The point is that some people think others who are sick have done something to "cause" the sickness. They are to blame.

In some cases that is true. Smoking causes cancer. If you smoke, you stand a chance of suffering intense pain while the cancer eats away at your lungs. If you drink alcohol constantly for years, you may suffer from a painful disease of the liver. Of course, cirrhosis of the liver strikes some people who do not drink alcohol. But the tendency is to think that those with cancer of the lungs or cirrhosis of the liver are to blame for their illnesses. "You did not care enough for me and our children to quit smoking. Now you are going to die and leave me with more than I can handle." If people do not say such things, they may think them and feel they have reason for thinking so. In response to this statement, Joan asked, "Are they not justified in thinking this way?"

"She didn't take care of herself. She smoked two packs of Camels a day."

"He didn't take his medicine."

"She thinks that walking to the table to eat is exercise."

"He ate enough Big Macs and fries every week to grease an eighteen-wheeler."

We cause some of our illnesses by the way that we live, but our illnesses are not always caused by something we did. Illness is not always a result of our actions, feelings, and thoughts. Yet one common response to suffering is to blame the one suffering for causing the sickness—and for causing so much trouble. When reviewing a manuscript of this book, Tom Shurling responded, "Blaming the victim is a way we control our fears of something happening to us. Saying the victim was in control allows us to think…that if we do X, we won't get sick." Also, there may be resentment of the person for getting sick and causing *us* all this trouble.

"You like being sick with everybody catering to your every wish and command. You are using your sickness to get your way. 'Bring me a sandwich.' 'Get me the paper.' 'Write the letter.' 'Pick up that blanket on the floor.' 'Sweep the floor. Vacuum the living room. Clean the bathroom. Wash the dishes.'"

Some people enjoy the power of pain and find it hard to give the power up, especially if they are powerless when physically or emotionally well. Some people use the power of sickness to get their way. That does not mean, however, that they are not hurting.

David Morris writes, "We use pain almost as regularly—and sometimes as cunningly—as pain uses us. The hope lies in learning how to use it for a better purpose."[3] Morris goes on to stress how people use pain:

> Patients, of course, use pain. Chronic pain...sometimes proves the best available means for resolving a conflict that might otherwise prove insolvable...The patient may take a perverse pride in being the most unfortunate, the longest suffering, and his friends may unwittingly encourage him to establish his worth in this way. One of our patients took delight in letting us know that all of his friends kept telling him, "I don't know how you do it."[4]

That response may be helpful to a friend who has to endure pain daily. It indeed gives them an identity. In this case, don't *blame the victim.*

Chapter 11

Responses That Hurt

All cultures and people need a reason for suffering. They try to understand why someone is suffering, so they grasp what is available in their culture, group, or religious tradition. Most people want to act compassionately, to demonstrate that they care for the suffering person and feel empathetically with him or her. They want the one suffering to know that they are hurting with them. When we try to help, we tell the sufferer that he or she is not alone in suffering.

Antoinette Bosco, who suffered deeply because of one family tragedy after another, describes her experiences with and approaches to suffering.[1] She writes that people have little patience with pat answers wrapped in what she calls "pop religiosity." "People don't know how to react to you or your troubles, so they tend to cover their ignorance by giving you nice and easy God talk." God talk, according to Bosco, uses the following phrases:

- Put everything in God's hands.
- Just do what Jesus would do.
- I know how you feel.
- God sends suffering to those God loves most.
- The back was made for the burden.

These and other phrases were not helpful to Bosco during her suffering, so she concludes that the phrases will not be helpful to others. Whether the phrases are helpful or not depends on the particular people and their religious and social experiences.

In my survey, the question "What did well-meaning people do that hurt you during your suffering?" brought some interesting responses. As you read these and other responses to those suffering, evaluate each phrase or action. Do you agree, disagree, or does it depend on the situation? (I will give you hints in italics about what I think of the phrases.)

- "God needed her more than we do."
  A lonely, selfish God with a mean streak.
- "It was God's will."
  God may be able to help us make sense out of the suffering, but God does not abuse people.
- "I know how you feel."
  I cannot know how another person feels even though I may have had a similar experience (i.e., death of a parent).
- "God is punishing you for something you did."
  I don't believe it.
- "It could be worse."
  How do you know?
- "Think of all the people who are worse off than you."
  Why?

A friend whose spouse died complained, "I get so tired of people telling me to count my blessings. They seem to think that because I don't have any money problems, I can count my money and attend teas, play bridge, and be happy. No amount of counting will bring Sid back."

What some people responding to the questionnaire may not have considered is that most of these phrases are attempts to help with the suffering. Because most people do not know what to say or do when a friend is suffering, they repeat the clichés of their church or club or culture. The clichés are attempts to help the one suffering cope with pain, whether the pain is physical, emotional, or spiritual.

Consider the responses to the question, "What could people who tried to help you have done better?" Eighty different sayings or phrases were given. *Only thirteen out of more than two hundred people were happy with what people said and did to and for them.* Following are some of their judgments:

1. Do not tell stories that relate to my illness.
2. Do not second-guess the doctors and prescribe alternative methods of treatment.
3. Talk less. You don't always have to say something to be helpful.
4. Listen more. Just be present. Don't offer solutions or reasons for suffering.
5. Don't blame the victim. Don't blame Satan. Don't blame God for my suffering.
6. Accept my feelings and avoid judgment.
7. Avoid the statement, "God doesn't give us more than we can handle."

The most frequently mentioned advice was to listen, *listen, LISTEN.* Don't try to solve my problems with your words. But such counsel goes against our need to help, our urge to do or say something to ease the pain. We should ask ourselves: *Am I saying this to help me cope with my suffering, or am I thinking about what is most helpful to my friend facing the fallout of chemotherapy?*

Sixty different bits of advice were given in response to the request, "List the best advice one can give to someone suffering." Here are a few of them. As you read these, remember that *what is the best advice to some is bad news to others.* The same words and actions do not meet the needs of all people in the same way. My own responses to several of these are in italics.

1. Don't say that God has a reason for my suffering.
2. Suffering is a way to discover that which no one can ever take away or destroy—God's presence.
3. You'll be a better person when this is over.
   Or a worse person.
4. Accept suffering as an old friend who comes around.
   I doubt that this person has suffered deeply.
5. Be patient, for this too will pass.
   That's easy for you to say.
6. God does not permit suffering, but he allows it in that God wants us suffering children to learn our lesson in life.
   This is confusing to anyone suffering—and to me.
7. Pray—Pray—Pray.

8. I'm sorry that you are suffering. I love you and I'm here for you.
9. Admit that you can't answer why, affirm the agony, ask what you can do, promise a prayer, read a psalm, find something to laugh about, or shut up and be present.
10. Walk beside me, hold hands, sit quietly, take a walk, listen, or give a puppy.

Our family has had puppies, rabbits, turtles, hamsters, and other pets while my children and I were growing up. I loved some of the pets more than others and still believe in the comfort and love pets give and receive. They can be a source of comfort for families and especially for those people who need an uncritical friend when they feel lonely or are hurting in other ways. However, I have a friend who is afraid of dogs. To give her a dog for comfort would do just the opposite; the puppy would compound her fears and tension. *What is helpful for one person may not be helpful for another.*

There is a basic element in responding to others when they are suffering. The Russian author Vladimir Nabokov offers us a clue to what this is in his response to others. His biographer writes:

> The key to Nabokov is that he loved and enjoyed so much in life that it was extremely painful for him to envisage losing all he held precious, a country, a language, a love, this instant, that sound. Nabokov insisted that in this life we have no choice but *to act as if another's pain is as real as our own.*[2]

Compassion is acting as if others' suffering is as real as our own—so far as that is possible. In so doing we try to communicate two things: (1) that we care and that it hurts us when our friend or loved one is hurting, and (2) that we believe God cares and is hurting with them. It is important for those suffering to believe that we believe in God's presence and compassion, for in tragic suffering, it is difficult for many people to believe in a God who would permit them to suffer that deeply. In response to the question "What is the best advice one can give to people suffering?" Alice wrote: "You are in my prayers—That helped a lot, especially when I couldn't pray for myself."

Tom Shurling, a psychologist and critic of this writing, summarized the thoughts of this chapter: "The struggle is how to find a way to be with a sufferer, to help meet their needs and to be an instrument of love, acceptance (grace). Advice giving, solution offerings, and simple chatter are signs of our own discomfort and fears. Sharing the walk (journey) is the objective. We cannot alter the course, but we can join them in their journey if only for a few minutes." He suggested asking a few questions:

- What can I do for you just now?
- Can you tell me what's going on in your life?
- What do you need?

These and similar questions give sufferers an opportunity, that is, permission, to talk about their pain or difficult life circumstances in coexisting with their suffering. Even if the people choose not to talk about themselves, the questions tell them that we care about them. They are the subject of the visit, not us.

Chapter 12

Trying to Make Sense of It

Catherine was in the hospital for a lung biopsy. She and I were concerned about the diagnosis. I decided to stay with her through the night. I would be there if she needed anything during the night and in case they took her to surgery early. I put the chair cushions on the floor and tried to sleep. The next morning, I picked up the medical chart at the foot of her bed. In big capital letters it read: ALERT HUSBAND IN ROOM. I looked at the words again and thought about how observant and sensitive these nurses were. I didn't think that they knew me that well. Then I looked back at the medical description. It said: ALERT! HUSBAND IN ROOM.

In the very confusing world of suffering, we try to read the signs to discover meaning in the tragedies we face with those we love. It makes a big difference in our lives and in the lives of those near to us how we interpret our suffering and theirs. It makes a difference where we put the exclamation points. We need to find meaning in suffering. When we respond to tragedy or suffering of any kind, we repeat sayings and thoughts that we discovered helped us make sense of otherwise senseless suffering.

The meaning we use to justify suffering must come out of experience to be helpful and to be believed. While on sabbatical leave from Lexington Theological Seminary, Catherine and I served for six weeks as "Theologians in Residence" in Kailua, Hawaii. We were furnished a five-bedroom house on a canal one block from the ocean. Each morning, while we were having our coffee out on the porch, ducks waddled up to greet us. During that February of 1992, we watched on television the terrible snowstorm in Lexington, Kentucky. While lounging in our summer shorts, we felt a touch of empathy for our friends in Lexington who had to deal with that weather.

During these months, I researched suffering, reading about Pearl Harbor, the Holocaust, Vietnam, spouse abuse, and other atrocities. When I reported my research to the faculty members, they burst out laughing. Their response was triggered by the incongruity of someone living in luxury and writing about suffering.

C. S. Lewis, a popular writer of fact and fiction, seems to write more in the realm of fiction than fact when he reasons,

> Now God, who has made us, knows what we are and that our happiness lays in Him. Yet we will not seek it in Him as long as He leaves us any other resort where it can even plausibly be looked for. While what we call "our life" remains agreeable we will not surrender to Him. What then can God do in our interest but make "our own life" less agreeable to us, and take away the plausible sources of false happiness. It is just here, where God's providence seems at first to be cruel, that the Divine humility, the stooping of the highest, must deserve our praise…Tribulations cannot cease until God either sees us remade or sees that our remaking is now helpless.[1]

Lewis' responses to, and explanations of, suffering in this statement are the following:

1. As long as we are not what God wants us to be, God will punish us "for our own good."
2. It is our fault that we suffer. "Don't blame God; you are the one causing the suffering."
3. When we get right with God, we will not suffer.
4. Sometimes God gives up on us, at which time the suffering will cease.

From this reasoning, we have to be either very good or very bad to avoid suffering. Lewis' book *The Problem of Pain* was clearly written by someone who was dealing with the problems of suffering intellectually from behind a lectern and a desk. When he wrote this very popular book, he had not stood at the side of a bed and held the hand of someone in intense pain. He had not experienced the confusion and helplessness one feels when watching a loved one grit his or her teeth, squeeze the eyes shut, tighten the muscles in the face, and grab the bedrails trying to keep from screaming.

Lewis has a long tradition behind him in his interpretation of suffering in *The Problem of Pain*. The authors of *What's a Christian to Do?* trace it back to a particular strand of scripture:

> One of the most powerful traditions within the Bible, the Deuteronomic tradition, regards evils that befall us as divine punishment for our sins (Deuteronomy 28:58–68). Hence, human sin is not only evil in itself, but is the ultimate source of other evils, such as human suffering, as well. God, of course, causes other evils, but in doing so reveals that God is not immoral, but moral, since it is good that sins are punished.[2]

After reading this, Tanya Tyler wrote, "Tell that to a suffering person!"

This type of thinking about God is not uncommon. A few years ago, a leading rabbi in Jerusalem outraged Holocaust survivors and secular Israelites by claiming that the Nazi genocide was God's punishment for sins such as violating the Jewish Sabbath and eating pork.

Let us return to C. S. Lewis. Later, Lewis fell in love and married. His spouse, Joy, was diagnosed with cancer. One of the most touching books ever written is his response to her condition. His emotions and thoughts about God, suffering, and relationships changed radically after he stood by Joy's bed as she struggled against cancer. Writing *A Grief Observed* was Lewis' way of dealing with his confusion and pain. He wrote to try to understand what was happening to him. He wanted to make sense out of this tragedy. He kept a journal, hoping to find meaning in a broken heart and a broken body. Listen to these words and feel the intensity of one who is hurting and is angry with people who speak thoughtlessly to him while he grieves.

What pitiable cant to say, "She will live forever in my memory!" *Live?*That is exactly what she won't do. You might as well think like the old Egyptians that you can keep the dead by embalming them. Will nothing persuade us that they are gone? What's left? A corpse, a memory, and (in some versions) a ghost. All mockeries or horrors. Three more ways of spelling the word *dead.* It was H. (his name for Joy) I loved. As if I wanted to fall in love with my memory of her, an image in my own mind! It would be a sort of incest.[3]

This is a different man from the one who wrote objectively about pain, about suffering. He confronts us with the following words about responding to suffering: "Talk to me about the truth of religion and I'll listen gladly. Talk to me about the duty of religion and I'll listen submissively. But don't come talking to me about the consolations of religion or I shall suspect that you don't understand."[4]

We want to help others when they are suffering. We try to relieve some of the pain by offering words that are supposed to aid the person suffering in understanding the reason for the suffering. Sometimes we succeed, and sometimes we fail.

June was a model student and daughter. She made the honor roll in school and was a cheerleader. June was thoughtful of others and well liked by most people, including her younger brother. June was killed in an automobile accident.

"It doesn't make sense," friends repeated to each other. Tears filled this small community, tears shed by both classmates and adults.

"Why? Why did June have to die?"

"God needed her more than we do," counseled an elderly woman. (Our reviewer Tanya's response to this was, "I would scream if someone ever said that to me in such a situation.")

As a pastor, it took all the repressive power I had not to theologically attack this cliché-carrying Christian. At the wake, people kept trying to make sense of this tragedy. They needed a reasonable explanation of it, even if they had to speak unreasonably. I put a notice in the newspaper announcing a seminar on death and grieving the following Wednesday evening. More than two hundred people showed up to either give or get answers to their questions about suffering. They were overwhelmed with shock, confusion, and grief. They were imprisoned in the present and had trouble seeing or feeling anything but their own and others' suffering.

Several years later, Jane Mayes, a lifelong friend, died. At the wake the night before the funeral Jane's children, Robbie, Libby, and Dickie, were greeting people as the people came to the casket. A friend of the family, David Underwood Sweet, summed up the moment when he said, "Good for her. Bad for us." Sometimes the pain of the moment blurs the hope of the resurrection. And other times the hope of the resurrection overcomes the shock of death and eases the pain of the loss of a mother or a child.

Chapter 13

The Shock Factor

One of the most difficult situations for many people is saying and doing something helpful for a person whose spouse has died. It is even more difficult when the couple is young and has a small child. When she was twenty-nine years old, Joyce Poole Harville's husband died. She shares her experiences of dealing with the loss and the ways people responded to her. Listen to her story and learn what not to say and do and what may be helpful when you or a friend has to deal with such grief. As we read this intimate confession, let's try to imagine saying something to her that would be helpful or doing something that might ease the pain. The following is Joyce's response to the suffering questionnaire, an interview, and our correspondence. She gives us a glimpse into her feelings, thoughts, and actions following her spouse's death.

George died around noon on Thursday, December 15, 1995. I was by his side in ICU, along with his mother, my pastor, a close friend, two chaplains, and a couple of nurses. I was the only one not crying. They escorted me to a little room with couches and a telephone so I could begin to make the necessary arrangements. I called family members and funeral homes and signed papers. I talked to doctors and a representative from the organ donation association without a crack in my voice or a tear in my eye. I was keenly aware of my behavior, my feelings, and the absence of the emotions

I was "supposed" to have. In a way, it was almost like an adrenaline rush. I had so much energy, even after only two hours of sleep the night before. I told my companions that I was considering driving the hundred miles back to my house. They convinced me otherwise. I remember feeling hungry and thinking how strange it was that I could think of food at a time like this. After the nurses removed all the tubes, I was invited to go back in and see George. I felt no sadness, no pain. I guess one could say that in some supernatural way, I was given the strength and the "cushion" from the pain that I needed to survive that day, to do all the things I had to do.

My pastor drove me home. On the way, we stopped at the funeral home, where my friend was one of the funeral directors. We talked about the embalming, about sending George's body home to Virginia for burial, about the expenses. Somewhere in the middle of this conversation I felt the blood drain from my head and reported that I thought I might pass out. A cold cloth kept me going until we were finished with the details. Then my pastor and the funeral director helped me out to the car for the rest of the drive home—still no tears, no real sadness, until I went to bed that night. In our bed I began to cry. I got up, sat on the floor, tore at my hair, and concealed a scream so I wouldn't wake the others in the house.

Upon arriving in Virginia the next day, I picked out a casket as if it were any other piece of wooden furniture. I'll never forget my reaction when our whole family went to the funeral home for a private viewing. I just stood there with my mouth open in disbelief while the others cried. George wasn't moving; he wasn't going to open his eyes or take my hand or speak to me or breathe. This was the first time I remember feeling angry. I wanted to throw things across the room, but I felt no desire to cry.

On the day of the funeral, my pastor escorted me into the church and sat beside me in the front row. I shook my head and said out loud, "This is not happening." Five days later, on Christmas Eve, after my son and almost everyone else had gone to bed, I went and sat in front of the Christmas tree. I screamed, "He's not coming back!" over and over again. Did it "hit me" then? Not really. After returning to Kentucky, to the house and the job and the routine, I would still catch myself saying to my son, "Let's go home and see...," and I would stop short of saying, "Daddy."

Six months after George's death, I was in the grocery store, picking out a snack that had caused many confrontations between George and me. I liked the chocolate ones; he preferred cinnamon. I stood in the grocery store with my hand on the cinnamon box for probably thirty seconds, saying to myself, "I don't have to buy these. George won't be here to eat them. I can buy the chocolate ones for myself." After finally convincing myself of this reality, I put the chocolate ones in the cart, paid for my groceries, and went home.

At the eight-month point, when I thought I was finally getting better, the nightmares began. It was obvious that my subconscious mind had not accepted the reality that George was gone. In the dreams, I mistakenly believed that George was dead. But then I discovered he was alive. My disbelief at seeing him in his casket played itself out in frightening ways in my sleep. Sometimes I would finish the dream believing he was alive. Then I would wake up. And the harsh reality would hit me in the face. The grief literature I read indicated that sleep disturbances often occur in the early stages of grief. Early on, I slept quite well, no dreams and felt rested. Again, I believe I was given what I needed so that I could function during that difficult time.

Throughout the process, friends and family members have observed the shock I experienced. At the hospital on the day of George's death, some people watched me carefully, waiting to catch me if I crashed. At the funeral home, some were frightened and upset by my apparent inability to conceive what was occurring. Some asked me questions like, "Can you believe this is happening?" Long-distance friends who waited several months to contact me after hearing the news confessed that they had to wait for their own shock and pain to subside. Many of these folks who have observed my grief are my colleagues in ministry, and like me, they have studied the stages of grief. Ministers know that some degree of shock and denial is a normal part of the process. But reading that in a textbook does not prepare us for the trauma. At a funeral I attended recently, the minister commented about the dignity and courage displayed by the widow. I wondered if he really knew better, or if I ought to approach him afterward and set him straight. I let it go and hoped he would be there for that widow in the weeks and months ahead.

Several folks have commented about the fact that I look like I am doing so well. They said that right after the funeral, when I came back to work, I looked like I never skipped a beat. I'm tempted to be angry with them for not being sensitive enough to see through my smile and recognize the pain. But others can only see what we allow them to see. I cannot be sure how much of my cheerful disposition was actual shock and how much was an award-winning performance. In reality, it was probably a combination of both. In the first month that I was back at work, I told a few folks that I thanked God for "the shock factor." In the moments when it would wear off, I was always grateful to have the shock return! I believe shock is a God-given safety net that helps us keep our sanity through unbearable pain. Despite how odd it feels at the time, and despite the comments of those who do not understand, I'm grateful for this stage of grief that allows the reality to sink in bit by bit, rather than all at once. One cannot stay in shock forever; the pain must be dealt with eventually. But the shock is nice while it lasts.

Becoming a widow at age twenty-nine presents a whole different set of issues older persons don't have to face. For example, no one tells an eighty-year-old, "You will get married again." But dozens of people have said those words to me. The first person to say this was my mother-in-law in the weeks after my husband's funeral. She made the comment with much anxiety, expressing her fear that if I married, she would be left out of her grandson's life. No matter how much I have tried to reassure her, this fear will probably remain.

Other people who say, "You will marry again," are saying this in a positive way, trying to give me hope. They want me to think that there will be positive things in my future. The only comment that has angered me at any point through this process was when a woman said, "I believe you'll have more children." For one thing, an issue that personal is none of her business; for another thing, she did not realize that I had no desire for more children even if my husband had lived. I simply felt as if we were meant to be a one-child family. The death of a loved spouse is a nightmare that could be unbearable. The shock factor, our friends, and our God support and comfort us while we suffer through the grief. Without the shock factor I would have suffered much more, so I thank God for that gift.

Chapter 14

The Language of Healing

The authors of *Speaking the Language of Healing* offer suggestions on how to think about breast cancer and how to talk with women with breast cancer. Their book will be helpful to all people who are dealing with a life-threatening illness. Jean Shinoda Bolen introduces us to this helpful book.

These four women found they were kindred souls who did not wish to live on a battlefield, define themselves as survivors, or become part of a cancer culture. They found that heroic stories could be depressing, that being in control was neither possible or desirable, and that they did not want to be drafted into the war against cancer. If anything, each found that cancer was a ticket to a deeper place on her spiritual, individual, human journey.

As those that investigate remissions know, in treatment of cancer of the breast, something works for someone, and nothing works for everyone. I think that this principle applies to psychological attitudes as well…What works for one woman doesn't work for every woman.[1]

Following is a chart entitled "How to Speak the Language of Healing."[2] It demonstrates what works for these four women and what should work for a large percentage of women with breast cancer. Whether these suggestions work for you or not, they stimulate us to decide how we want to think and talk about breast cancer and other major illnesses.

How to Speak the Language of Healing

Instead of saying	Say
I am a victim of breast cancer.	I was diagnosed with breast cancer on__.
I am a survivor.	I am a cancer initiate. I am living with a breast cancer diagnosis. It has been six years since my initial diagnosis.
I am fighting breast cancer.	I am in treatment for breast cancer.
I beat cancer.	I was initiated by cancer.
She lost her battle with breast cancer.	Breast cancer was the cause of her death.
The war on cancer.	Advances in breast cancer research and treatment.
Chemotherapy is poison.	Chemotherapy is medicine.
How are you?	It's good to see you.
I am cured of cancer.	I am doing well.
Anything about God such as, "God must love you very much."	I will keep you in my thoughts. I will keep you in my prayers.
You'll be fine.	I hope it went well.
Is there anything I can do?	Be specific in your offers: Can I get your groceries, pick up your kids?

What these authors did was tell us how to talk to them about their suffering. The vocabulary causes us to think about people with cancer and the many issues surrounding cancer. For instance, while reading the book, I relived the struggle my mother and all of us who loved her had with the mystery of cancer. We did not know how to talk to her or about the disease in the 1950s. If you are suffering, it may be helpful to make a list similar to the one given here.

Talking about major illnesses reminds me of an incident that occurred in Mayfield, Kentucky, where I was the pastor of First Christian Church. I entered the hospital room of the teenaged daughter of the church's board chair. After greeting Jim, her father, I asked Jill why she was in the hospital. She told me she was having her appendix taken out. We talked a few minutes, I prayed, and I left the room. Jim followed me outside the room. I said, "At least it's not major surgery." Jim quickly asked me if I knew the difference between major and minor surgery. When I did not answer, he explained, "Major surgery is when it's your daughter."

It makes a big difference how we talk about cancer and other illnesses. The preceding authors gave us some specific suggestions based on sound principles when thinking and talking about breast cancer. The principles are applicable to other illnesses, major and "minor."

Responses to Suffering: Listening, Thinking, and Doing Compassion

Chapter 15

Which God Do You Choose?

An answer to suffering involves both God and people. God works in community, through people, to offer us comfort and meaning when we suffer. To experience understanding that communicates compassion, we need someone else to hear and respond. We need community. We need the church, a group of people who have dedicated themselves to caring for one another and for those who are not a part of the church. We need God, either explicitly or implicitly. "Where God is, love is, and where love is, God is." So when people care for us unconditionally, God is present, whether we believe it or they believe it, or not.

There is continued confusion about God's power and God's compassion. Dorothee Soelle captures this theological conflict when she writes, "Whenever people are confronted by senseless suffering, faith in a God who embodies both omnipotence and love has to waver or be destroyed."[1]

Some people choose to go with God's "macho power"–an all-powerful God who is in charge of all pain and joy. They choose a God who justifies their actions of destruction. In 1998, the Kentucky state legislature voted into law that a minister may carry a concealed weapon in a church building. A minister lobbied for the law. He said, "Little is sacred in these dangerous times." That is why he believes that ministers should be allowed to carry pistols beneath their robes. His rationale for the law was that whenever someone came to rob the congregation of its money, he could shoot it out with the robber. Of course, he did not say it that way. He said, "This law will send a message to all people who even think about robbing the church." That message is: Do not expect us to care about you, and if you try to use power to get our goods, we will shoot you.

This action and the pastor's words are embarrassing to Christians and to the citizens of the Commonwealth of Kentucky. If we perceive God as the all-powerful, ultimate terminator of our enemies, we have a problem with God's compassion. If God carries a gun to church to blow away God's and our enemies, we cannot conceive of a God who "forgives our sins" and accepts us in our suffering.

If we have problems with God's compassion, we probably find it difficult to believe in people's motivation for acting with love. Following his speech "Pacifism and Its Problems," Leo Rosten was approached by a "pink-cheeked, beaming little dowager, who looked as if she had stepped right off the cover of a Mother's Day Candy Box. She addressed me with the utmost kindliness: 'Any man who goes around saying God's children are capable of the horrid things you described should be stood up against a blank wall and shot dead.'"[2] Can we separate God's compassion from people's compassion? The answer to that question depends on one's beliefs about God and people. Can we separate God's power from people's power?

We cannot have it both ways. Either God is all-powerful in the worldly, macho sense or all-loving in the creative, compassionate sense. In the ancient and modern worlds, macho-type power is the power to punish those who do not do as we wish. It is an athletic, patriarchal concept that parades itself as a virtue. Some people cannot conceive of a God who is not in control of every aspect of the world, for the lack of power is considered a weakness. These people think and feel that they need an all-powerful God to win the final battle between good and evil by defeating the enemy in some supernatural way. The disciples who stood at the foot of the cross felt the same type of confusion. "Forgive them, for they know not what they do" was not the response they expected from their Savior. They wanted God to slay their enemies in the old-fashioned way, with the power and style of a dominating dictator.

When we need to be in control, to be superior, to dominate others, to win at all costs, it is difficult to choose a compassionate

God over a military-type God. Therefore, when God does not rescue us from suffering with some kind of miracle, we become disillusioned and often afraid.

Suffering is always a theological faith issue because it creates feelings of being abandoned. The disciples felt abandoned when Jesus was crucified. If we choose to believe that God is a compassionate God instead of a macho-style Savior, we may feel betrayed as well as abandoned when we suffer radically. Even when hit with the horrors of prolonged pain, Christians often respond in unusual ways because their faith is still a part of them.

"My faith is shot to hell," confessed Mack, whose spouse had died a year before. "But I still pray every night and several times a day."

In *The Trial Of God*, Elie Wiesel wrote that he witnessed three rabbis who decided one winter to indict God for allowing children to be massacred. "When the trial was over and God found guilty, the rabbis realized that it was time for prayers so they bowed their heads to pray."[3] In the face of the horror of horrors, the rabbis still felt the need to stay in contact with God. They struggled with the problems created when one chooses between God's macho power and God's power of compassion.

When we decide to let go of the idea that God is all-powerful, omnipotent in the worldly sense of power, we are free to love a God worthy of loving. Once that leap of faith grasps us, we are on our way to a little understanding of suffering. As Soelle claims, "The Christian faith relates to suffering not merely as remover or consoler. It offers no *'supernatural remedy for suffering,' but strives for supernatural use of it."*[4]

In *What's a Christian to Do?* the authors write:

After every tragedy, God begins immediately the process of healing, not through a unilateral intervention in the world, but through a persuasive call to our world to transform itself. Thus, although God never quits, so to speak, on evils that beset us, God is dependent on our cooperation for effective resistance to them.[5]

God is involved in the healing process, often using us to help the one suffering.

Wendy Farley offers the idea of divine compassion as a healing response to suffering. The following quotes will not do justice to her concept of divine compassion, but will offer some insights for our reflection.

- Compassion as empowering presence is the sublime and holy power of mercy, comfort, justice, and redemption.
- Compassion is the intensity of divine being as it enters into suffering, guilt, and evil to mediate the power to overcome them. As human beings and communities apprehend the presence of divine compassion for them and with them, they experience power to resist the degrading effects of suffering, to defy structures and policies that institutionalize injustice and to confront their own guilt.
- Divine compassion is not mercy to sinners at the end of time but the fight for life in all times.
- Divine compassion is directed toward the restoration of wholeness and freedom in all aspects of creation.[6]

When people are traumatized by a tragedy and pain drives deeply into their souls, a spiritual crisis is caused by feeling abandoned not only by God but often by people. At that moment, words of affection and affirmation seldom eliminate feelings of being alone. But the continuing presence of people who care about us eventually breaks through and gives us a sense of being part of a loving family.

Ideally, in our Christian community we are accepted for who we are even when we do not accept ourselves–affirmed as worthy human beings when we feel worthless, understood when we do not understand ourselves, forgiven when we feel guilty, and loved when we feel unlovable. So healing from suffering, as far as possible in a particular situation, occurs through faith in God and in relationships with people in a faith community who project hope for a better future when we feel hopeless. In this community, the clergy do not carry weapons to shoot those who are in need of money and in need of a God of compassion.

Viktor Frankl, a psychiatrist from Vienna, spent years in Nazi prison camps trying to cope with impossible living conditions and to find meaning in that inhuman setting. His father, mother, brother, and spouse died in the camps or were murdered in the gas ovens. Only Frankl and his sister survived the war. Frankl wrote of his thoughts in the midst of this senseless suffering:

> For the first time in my life I saw the truth, as it is set into song by so many poets, proclaimed as the final wisdom by so many thinkers. The truth is that love is the ultimate and highest goal to which [people] can aspire. Then I grasped the meaning of the greatest secret that human poetry and human thought and belief have to impart: the salvation of man is through love and in love.[7]

That response to suffering is far more powerful than one that tries to conquer the enemy with macho, military power. It is the power of compassion given by the God of compassion.

Chapter 16

Compassion 101

My friend Dabney Parker tells about a sign her parents kept on the wall in their kitchen. It read, "Life is hard yard by yard, but inch by inch it is a cinch." This saying oversimplifies suffering, but it reminds us to try to stay focused on the present and handle problems one at a time. Do not get overwhelmed by everyone and everything that seems to demand an immediate solution. Do not assume that all problems can be solved to your satisfaction. Do not expect life to be pain-free and easy. Learn to deal with suffering in your own way. Dabney's parents seem to be saying, "We try to deal with the little things in life as they come along; we don't put off handling problems until they accumulate and become too hard to manage."

In *A Fleeting Sorrow*[1] we witness a person's response to being diagnosed with a life-threatening disease. The author's description follows. Paul, forty years old, was told that he had lung cancer. (He was a heavy smoker.) He tried to deny the fact; he did not want to believe the X rays, but the evidence stared him in the face. His reaction amazed him. For the first time he understood the lies, the refusals to accept the evidence that he had so often witnessed among his friends and acquaintances. His death would come as a shock to him and him alone, he kept thinking. People would be surprised by it; those who loved him would surely grieve. But death would not shock anyone the way today's news had shocked him. He felt rejected, ridiculed, debased. Yes, debased; that was the word.

94

But–and he was sure of this–those who had loved him or looked up to him until now, some for as long as thirty years, his friends, lovers, or merely passing fancies, as soon as they knew he was sick, would start avoiding him, because he had been misleading them all these years. They would feel sorry for him, of course, but they would also shy away from him. He dreaded being thought of as a fraud; he had been *acting* like a healthy person. What about all those cases that he had heard about, incomprehensible and little understood–especially by the doctors and specialists, to be sure–where people who had been given only a short time to live had defied all the predictions by living for another twenty or thirty years? He would go to Lourdes and pray for a miracle. This is an understandable reaction to news of terminal illness.

Paul searched from one end of Paris to the other for someone who would truly miss him. He looked for "immortality" from a former spouse to the chef of the restaurant where he was a regular customer. Paul talked to anyone who would listen. Anyone who would remember him and miss him would assure him of a form of eternity. Paul felt humiliated and guilty, two feelings he disliked most. It was true that the worst of this was not that he was going to die in six months, but that he was painfully aware of it. He had been given the news of his death in a cold, impersonal way. Paul thought the way he was told of his terminal illness was a crying shame: Compassion should be an obligatory part of any doctor's education and baggage. They should have a course called "Compassion 101– Compassion and all its various implications."

After a full day of searching for something, a day of reflections on his life, a day of reviewing his relationships, a day of emotions that fought to be denied–fear, guilt, shame, greed, jealousy, anger, hostility, love or something like love– the phone rang. It was the doctor. The doctor explained that there had been a mistake in the laboratory and that Paul did not have cancer of the lungs. Paul was angry and relieved.

Would he have felt less desperate or hurt more if he had had lung cancer? I think not. Perception is so important. What we think affects how we feel and behave.

Let us look at how Paul responded to the news of his forthcoming death.

1. Paul prayed for a miracle. He wanted a miraculous healing. When told we have a terminal illness, we often pray and hope for a miraculous cure. "Anoint me and make me well." "Lower me into the healing waters of Lourdes." "Smuggle the new experimental drug in from South America."

2. Paul focused on the past. He wanted to know that he had made a difference in the lives of others. When faced with chronic suffering or impending death, some people dwell on the past and others focus on the future. Some people review their lives and replay the incidents that were significant to them, both good and bad. When faced with bypass surgery in 1987, I did not think about the past. I thought about the future. It bothered me that Catherine would have to deal with all the problems that would come with raising three sons alone. I did not want to miss all the celebrations that would come with raising three sons. I also did not want to miss the celebrations with Catherine that would come with the empty nest. When diagnosed with cancer or heart disease or some other potentially life-threatening illness, some people focus on the future.

3. Paul was concerned about what people would think of him after his death. Some people prepare their own funerals, writing every word and detail of the ritual. They want to be remembered in a particular way. They usually want people to remember the good and forget the bad. Close friends smile knowingly as the process of self-anointed sainthood is announced in the words of the deceased. Fortunately, God is also smiling, and, I imagine, thinking, *How could Michael have heard about my grace all those years and never caught the spirit of it?* It is normal to want people to think well of us, even after we are no longer around to try to prove how smart or compassionate or charming or skilled we were. Catherine Broadus and Nell Waldrop read obituaries just to see what people put in

print about themselves. Following are a few descriptions to make the point.

- "John was an avid Wildcat fan." This was in the *Lexington Herald-Leader* newspaper. In Kentucky, basketball is extremely important. Some believe being a University of Kentucky basketball fan is a ticket into heaven or the next best thing.
- "Barry made a hole in one." This is a special accomplishment for a golfer.
- "Mary loved everyone." Everyone?
- "Bessie held every office in the church." That surely must qualify Bessie for the kingdom.

4. Paul needed someone to understand him. He did not want pity; he wanted someone to care. Paul did not want people to avoid him because he was going to die. It is not uncommon for some to abandon those who are suffering, because they do not know how to deal with the suffering of someone close to them. They may avoid the sick person because they do not want "anything that heavy laid on them." There is a type of healing that comes with understanding and caring.

This idea is captured in a short story entitled "A Small, Good Thing" by Raymond Carver.[2] Ann ordered a birthday cake for Scotty. The old baker listened carefully as she described the space scene she wanted for her son, whose birthday was Monday. He promised that the cake would be ready Monday morning. On the way to school Monday, Scotty and a friend tossed a potato chip bag back and forth as they walked. Scotty stepped into the street to catch the bag. A car hit him. Scotty lay in the street a few minutes, then he got up and, without answering his friend's questions, walked home. He told his mother what had happened. Ann was listening to Scotty as he went limp. The ambulance arrived and took him to the hospital. The doctor reassured Ann and Howard that Scotty was all right, that he would be out of the deep sleep shortly. During the next two days, Scotty had several tests but still remained unconscious. At eleven o'clock the first night, Howard left the hospital to go home to bathe and rest a few minutes. As soon as he opened the door, the phone rang.

"There's a cake here that wasn't picked up," the voice said.

Howard did not know what the man was talking about. The man did not believe him and hung up the phone. While Howard was in the tub, the phone rang again. Thinking it might be the hospital calling, Howard hauled himself out of the tub, grabbed a towel, and rushed to answer the phone. The caller hung up. The next day, Ann finally went home to bathe and change clothes. The phone rang. It was the same weird person on the other end of the line talking about a cake. Ann hung up the phone.

Although not a common practice for them, Ann and Howard prayed. They prayed for Scotty to be well.

Wednesday, after all the reassurances of the doctors that Scotty would be all right, Scotty died. When Ann and Howard arrived home, the phone rang.

"Your Scotty, I got him ready for you," the man's voice said. "Did you forget him?"

Ann cursed the evil man. Then she realized who was calling. *How could anyone be so cruel as to joke about a child's suffering?* thought Ann. She and Howard drove to the shopping center to get even with the old man for his cruelty. The mall was closed. They looked in the window of the bakery and saw a light. They went to the back of the mall. They pounded on the door. When the baker opened the door and saw who it was, he offered them the three-day-old cake for half price. This angered the grieving parents even more. Ann and Howard had found a convenient target for their anger. They cursed the baker. He was hammered with hostility born of fear, frustration, anger, and anxiety. He got "bashed" for all the pain caused by the doctors, an automobile driver, and God.

After the man learned of Scotty's death and asked for forgiveness, Ann and Howard accepted the coffee and warm roll the baker gave them. Then they listened to the old baker tell his story, the story of a lonely old man who worked sixteen hours a day. They listened and ate "a small, good thing" until the sun came up. The mother, father, and old man continued to talk and listen and care.

A type of healing came in that small, hot bakery back room. Venting their hostility and then listening to the painful problems of an old man transformed Ann's and Howard's preoccupation with their tragedy into acts of compassion for a man who cared about what had happened to them. Neither the time with the baker nor their prayers brought Scotty back, but sharing in the life of a lonely man did help the parents deal with the loss. Compassion comes through understanding. Understanding comes from listening and trying to feel with the one suffering. It is important for us to understand our suffering, and it is equally important to us for someone else to try to understand our suffering. Their acceptance of us helps us accept who we are when suffering.

When tragedy strikes and suffering threatens to overcome us, we sometimes search the past for a form of redemption. Other times we look to the future, hoping to have a chance to live our dreams and fulfill our responsibilities. The church promises that God understands this—we know this because of the cross—and that God's people are called to try to understand and respond to one another's suffering. This gives meaning to the suffering for the one suffering and for the one feeling with the sufferer. Scotty, his parents, and the old baker point to one way of dealing with our suffering—sharing it with caring people.

Chapter 17

God's Endorphin for the Heart

The Christian Men's Fellowship met at Christmount Assembly Grounds in the Black Mountain area of North Carolina. I had been invited to be the speaker for this weekend gathering of more than two hundred men. Translated, that means that I was the excuse for these men to get together in the mountains and have renewal time through conversation, worship, and recreation. After the first session, some people hiked in the mountains, others told tales while watching the hummingbird enjoy the birdfeeder, and some played softball. I was playing softball, covering right field, which was on a rising hill. The batter hit a short pop fly ball. I charged down the hill, keeping my eye on the ball. When I hit the level ground, the speed and shock of the impact threw me forward into the air. When I hit the ground, my feet were above my head. My chest landed on my right elbow. It felt as if a hot poker were piercing my chest and lungs. I tried to play for a few more minutes, but had to give up. Back in the motel room a physician, who was one of the softball players, examined me. He assured me that my ribs seemed to be in place.

That night I hobbled to the meeting room where I was to give a speech. The pain was intense. After being introduced, I shuffled to the lectern, stepped up on the platform, and began to make the presentation. I was hurting. Gradually, I became absorbed in the speech. Later, while answering questions, I paced back and forth on the platform as erect as a Marine. I was excited about what was happening. It was a stimulating time. I was having fun, and not once did I think about the pain. However, when the session was over and I started walking off the platform, the pain shot through my chest, and the hot poker almost did me in. The next morning, driving back to Lexington, I continued to gasp for breath. I took two aspirin without water and almost choked. The pain intensified.

After arriving in Lexington, I decided that since there was not anything seriously wrong with me, I would wait until my annual medical checkup to ask my doctor, Dr. James Orr, about my injury. The appointment was eight days later.

"Loren, you are in good health, except for one thing," Dr. Orr told me. "Evidently, in some way you broke a rib and it pierced a lung, causing it to collapse. The strange thing is that the rib bounced back to its original position. The lung is half filled up; the body is trying to repair the damage. Let's give it two weeks to see if it will complete the task." It did.

Endorphins are the body's natural morphine for physical pain. The body produces the painkiller to help us cope with pain. It distracts the mind from the source of pain. While giving the speech, I did not feel the pain; my mind and body took over to offer the relief needed at that time. Creativity and compassion help us to forget ourselves; we focus on someone or something else.

Compassion is the endorphin for our suffering with and for others. By losing ourselves in other people's problems, we forget ourselves for a while. When we are suffering, compassion gives us a break from our pain. Compassion is God's prescription for egoism and apathy.

Let's continue to examine the characteristics of compassion. Ruby died of lung cancer at the age of forty-five. Ruby's spouse, Jack, reflected,

> I leaned over in the coffin and fixed her fingers so the nicotine stains wouldn't show. Ruby had the creamiest soft skin and I hated to have brown spots ruin her for people. Suppose you went to view somebody who'd died being shot or stabbed somewhere so you'd notice. Don't you know they'd fill in with some kind of spackle and smooth it over to match him?[1]

Compassion is caring for and doing something for others, even when they cannot return the favor or write a thank-you note. Jack cared about what people thought of Ruby, even as she lay in the coffin. He wanted them to remember her, not as a smoker who killed herself but as a person loved by her family and friends.

People respond to those who are suffering in different ways. We respond individually to specific people. Then we unite and are helpful in a different way. We cooperate so that together we can do more than we could do by ourselves. The Christian Church (Disciples of Christ) has a program called The Week of Compassion (WOC). Its many projects of caring are funded by an annual offering from people through their congregations. The program works with other churches through Church World Service, an agency in the World Council of Churches. The current director, the Reverend Johnny Wray, writes:

> The WOC has already responded to or is now responding to El Niño-related disasters in Bolivia, Ecuador, and Peru; the ice storms in New England and Quebec; the hunger crisis in North Korea; the massacre in Chiapas, Mexico; typhoon destruction in the Pacific; floods in the Congo, Kenya, and India; earlier storms in Florida, Texas, North Carolina, Kentucky, and Tennessee; humanitarian emergencies in Bulgaria, Iraq, and Chechnya; earthquakes in China and Afghanistan—and the year is not yet two months old.[2]

This way of responding to those in pain is admirable and much needed. However, to know the meaning of life as revealed in the biblical sense, we cannot simply give money so that others may live a little easier and never bother to get involved personally with specific people. To be fully human, we have to feel for, and respond to, another person's suffering.

Just as suffering engages the whole person physically, emotionally, mentally, and spiritually, compassion as a creative response to the one suffering engages the whole person. Here are some ways compassion works:

Relief from self-indulging empathy comes from doing something. "Otherwise we would only offer condescending charity that reaches down from on high. We can only help sufferers by stepping into their time frame,"[3] trying to empathize with them—to feel *with* them and not feel simply *for* them.

Thinking of ways to be helpful is a challenge for some people and natural for others. It may be as simple as reading the newspaper to a friend who has had cataract surgery or as complicated as discovering ways to relate to one's mother who has Alzheimer's disease.

Listening to a person confess fears of the pain that awaits him or her in the next medical procedure (cancer treatment, etc.), or feeling the agony of the father who has lost a son in an automobile accident is a spiritual gift. Helping people make some sense out of tragedy is a spiritual offering.

Writing about undeserved suffering, which includes that of war veterans, prisoners of war, battered women, and incest victims, Judith Lewis Herman addresses the "why me?" question:

> In order to develop a full understanding of the trauma story, the survivor must examine the moral questions of guilt and responsibility and reconstruct a system of belief that makes sense of her undeserved suffering. Finally, the survivor cannot reconstruct a sense of meaning by exercise of thought alone. The remedy for justice also requires action. The survivor must decide to do what is to be done.[4]

Being a part of this process, whether it is our own trauma or that of a friend, is a spiritual exercise.

The authors of a book entitled *Compassion* have a more limited definition of the word. "The word compassion is derived from the Latin words *pati* and *cum,* which together mean 'to suffer with.' Compassion asks us to go where it hurts, to enter into places of pain, to share in brokenness, fear, confusion, and anguish."[5] That is the way we normally think of compassion, but it is a limited view. We cannot separate our feelings so easily—pain is often touched by love, and sadness is softened by joy. To open ourselves to the suffering of a person and not reach for the joy and happiness in that person is to limit both of us in the healing process.

We will continue to explore compassion as a response to suffering. The following are responses to the question: "What do people do or say that is helpful to those suffering?" Here are attempts to express compassion:

1. "'You are in my prayers.' That helped a lot, especially when I couldn't pray for myself," one person explained. (This deserves repeating.)
2. "The idea that someone took time to be with me was the best gift. It was the presence that mattered the most, not the words or prayers."
3. "Be close to God, believe in yourself, lean on friends, seek to do things that take you out of yourself, speak your fears to a confidant, pray for comfort, courage, insight, and hope."
4. "Even now, having lost so much, I'm not so sure I would know what to say to someone who is hurting. I would simply cry with them and hope my own pain would be lessened in the process."
5. "Find a friend and share your feelings." (This was one of the most mentioned suggestions for those suffering. Remember that the people responding are "advising" out of their own experiences of suffering.)

As noted earlier, the words spoken and the actions taken in response to someone suffering may or may not be helpful in a particular situation. It depends on the person's and your experiences with people, churches, and organizations. At church a woman said to another church member who had just undergone chemotherapy treatment for cancer, "Think about it; things could be worse."

Though spoken in an attempt to help, she in essence said, "Quit complaining! Think about how lucky you are to have a husband who cares about you and how you are still able to come to church, and so on." I do not think that right after someone has had chemotherapy is the time to reprimand them for complaining about having cancer. Making someone feel guilty for being sick usually does not help the person get well or feel better. A prayer, a hug, an arm around the shoulders, a listening ear, and a box of chocolate-covered cherries may be a better way to help.

Chapter 18

Warm Hands

Catherine and Mabel exercised at the Aquatic Club. Afterward, while sitting in the donut shop, Catherine started telling Mabel about visiting a person in the Julius Marks Home, which was for people who did not have any other place to go for help with health problems. As soon as Catherine started describing the problems of this woman, Mabel said, "Don't lay anything that heavy on me this early in the morning." It was eleven o'clock.

Mabel did not want to have her good feelings contaminated by anything sad. She did not want to think about or feel anything unpleasant. We can understand that. It would be nice if we never had to think about suffering. If only we could turn our heads, ignore the problem, and wish the pain away, ignore the suffering and live as if the Julius Marks Home and the people in it did not exist.

We cannot compartmentalize compassion. We cannot say, "I will feel sorry for Tom tomorrow at six o' clock," and turn off our feelings for him the remainder of the day. We either have the capacity for compassion or we do not. Wendy Farley calls compassion an enduring disposition.[1] Maybe Mabel merely wanted to avoid thinking about unpleasant things at that time of the day. Maybe she is a very compassionate person most of the time, and that was not a good day or time for Mabel to carry another load of empathy on her heavy heart.

Later, after Catherine had a lung biopsy, Mabel phoned Catherine to tell her that she could not come to see her in the hospital because Dawahare's clothing store was having a sale. Some people are not conditioned to feel for others. Compassion is not a natural emotion for them. Compassion is not an enduring disposition for them. Even if they notice others suffering, they think about how inconvenient it is for them. *They* remain the subjects, not the ones suffering.

We can take a break from thinking about and feeling for friends and family who are suffering and still have an enduring disposition of compassion. Because we do not think about mother's loss of memory twenty-four hours a day does not mean that we do not love her. We must find ways to renew ourselves in order to have the strength and sensitivity to be genuinely helpful. In *Forgetting Whose We Are: Alzheimer's Disease and the Love of God,* David Keck describes a condition caregivers develop from having to care constantly for an Alzheimer's patient. *Acedia* is weariness in welldoing.[2] No matter how much we love someone, we can get weary and worn-out from the constant demands on our emotions, minds, and bodies. We need to develop the ability to live in the moment and to find ways of renewing ourselves. This is much easier to recommend than to do.

When I am laughing with my grandson, Christian, nothing else exists in the world. When I am with Catherine on special occasions, nothing else exists in the world. There are ways to escape the pain of the present, to take a break from the empathy that threatens to exhaust us emotionally and spiritually.

Instead of helping us, our religious beliefs may trap us into believing that we must suffer constantly with people in order to live our faith. Simone Weil, a social activist and mystic, was such a person. She has been revered by such people as T. S. Eliot, who described Weil as "one who might have been a saint." Andre Gide saw her as the most spiritual writer of the century. Albert Camus called her "the only great spirit of our time."[3] I disagree with all these famous, intelligent people and many of my friends who think highly of Weil. She may have been a saint, but if so, she was a pathological one. Yet God can use her and our pathology to help others.

Read and think about the implications of the following words she wrote.

"Love of God is pure where joy and suffering inspire an equal degree of gratitude."
[*Thank you, God, for my grandfather's sexual abuse, Auschwitz, and cancer.* In response to this idea, one of the reviewers of this book, Becky Brown, wrote, "Jesus prayed, 'Let this cup pass.' I do not believe Jesus was grateful for the cross."]

"If we love God while thinking that he does not exist, he will manifest his existence."
[*I don't believe in you, God, but I love you.*]

"Every time I think of the crucifixion of Christ I commit the sin of envy."[4]
[*Hurt me, God, to prove you love me*]

Weil did much good and has inspired many people. She gave up an easy life for one of hardship to identify with the poor. She starved herself to death when a telephone call could have kept her alive to continue trying to help the poor. She lived by the slogan, "I suffer, therefore I am." She could not take a break from her suffering long enough to be renewed by the loving spirit of God.

German theologian Dorothee Soelle captures the essence of Weil when she writes, "The meaning of the cross and the resurrection, failure and victory, weeping and laughter, makes the utopia of a better life possible for the first time. He who does not weep needs no utopia; to him who only weeps God remains mute."[5] In order to survive to help others another day, we must find ways to renew ourselves emotionally and spiritually.

Because some people have not learned how to be sensitive to those who are suffering does not mean that they cannot perform acts with a compassionate touch. Some doctors need "sensitivity" training in this area. Catherine was lying in the hospital bed waiting on the wise words from the physician pertaining to her upcoming cardiac catheterization. Dr. "Insensitivity" stood by the bed and said solemnly, "Now, honey, you go home and get your affairs in order. Check your will; be sure it is as you want it. And remember, if anything goes wrong, it would have happened anyway." This happened in 1998 in Lexington, Kentucky, not 1888 in the backwoods office of some undertrained quack. This doctor had the audacity not only to suggest that Catherine might die, but that if she did, it was not his fault. God is in charge of such things, that is, in this doctor's mind. That is not only terrible theology but atrocious bedside manner.

In the spring of 1996, the University of Florida announced a new position on the medical school staff. Dr. Robert Watson was given a position that challenged him to teach medical students how to provide compassionate patient care. "We believe medicine is as much art as science," he said. "We want to make sure our medical students graduate with the ability to communicate effectively and compassionately with their patients."[6]

While it is very difficult to change what a person feels, education can change the way one relates to others. People can be trained to listen and perform particular acts that help others. Notice the concern and sensitivity of the following doctor.

> Before visiting a patient in our poorly heated hospital, Gwynne Williams would place his hand on a radiator, or immerse it in hot water. Sometimes he walked the wards with his right arm tucked Napoleonically inside a large coat, concealing the hot water bottle that made his hand a good listener. A cold hand would cause a reflex tightening of the patient's abdominal muscles, but a warm, comforting hand coaxed them to relax.[7]

That is sensitivity that communicates compassion. It can and should happen anywhere that the opportunity presents itself.

I took my 1995 Buick LeSabre to Glenn Buick to have the left-turn indicator fixed. The waiting room looked like most automobile waiting rooms. There were eleven reasonably comfortable chairs and a coffee machine offering regular and decaffeinated coffee, fake cream, and sugar. On the wall hung four pictures of golf holes, decorated with manicured fairways and greens, and pink and yellow flowers. Four men and one woman sat in the chairs waiting for their cars to be repaired.

Two men were especially talkative. They were friendly people in a public place—not always a common occurrence.

"Did you see that TV program on car safety last night?" one man asked. None of us had. He proceeded to tell us how near to death we were whenever we got in our Buicks. He smiled and laughed the whole time he described our fate.

"I was in a car that was totaled in 1993," Frank said. The car collapsed around him. The Jaws of Life had to be used to get him out of the wreck. That car was a Buick, and it protected him from certain death.

I probed a little. Frank proceeded to talk about his medical problems. In 1987, Frank was injured at work. The vertebrae in his neck and the upper part of his spine were smashed. The surgeons took two ribs and four inches of bone from his legs to try to rebuild his spine. He was in the hospital for nineteen months. Surgeons from several states came to Lexington to study this experimental procedure. When Frank entered the hospital, he was six feet tall. When he left the hospital, he was five feet eight inches tall. The automobile accident in 1993 complicated his spinal injury.

Frank wore a neck collar. He was in constant pain twenty-four hours a day. He had morphine to take in times of unbearable pain. He refused to let the doctors put a pump in to regulate doses of morphine every four hours. He took one pill a day when he needed it most.

"I don't want to give up the little bit of control of my life that I have left," he explained.

After listening to this story for thirty minutes, I said, "This is so terrible I have a feeling that you are putting me on." I smiled when I said it. He reassured me that everything he told us was true; he had been in constant pain for the past six years.

"I guess it's just not my time yet," he said with a sigh of resignation.

I almost forgot to tell you...Frank had another automobile accident three months ago, again hurting his spine. Frank explained, "My back and neck feel like an abscessed tooth all the time."

This man responded to pain by talking about it wherever people would listen. He needed to talk about his neck collar and the chronic pain. He needed someone to be interested in him, even in public places. Frank needed someone to say, "That must be very painful. I don't understand how you stand it." All but one person in the waiting room listened and encouraged him to talk about his suffering. Strange as it seems, this automotive waiting room became a caring community. God does not need a steeple to create a community of compassion.

That kind of listening and acting can be taught in the church, in medical schools, in social work colleges, and in the workplace. And it should be. We should not wait until a sexual harassment or racial discrimination lawsuit is filed to teach people how to be sensitive to the feelings and needs of others.

We are created with the capacity for compassion. Early in life, that spark of caring is either sabotaged or nurtured. How we respond to others is conditioned by those early life experiences. The "enduring disposition" is the gift of caring; it does not pick the place or person for expressions of compassion. Sometimes it happens in an automotive waiting room. Other times it happens in a donut shop while two people sip coffee and munch a donut after exercise, but not with Mabel around.

Chapter 19

The Gift of Compassion

"Suffering is our emotional response to pain."[1] Our emotions are not easily separated from the pain of cancer when it eats away at our bodies. Our bodies hurt; our stomachs ache; our lungs sting; and the fire in our bellies will not go out. That is not just a physical sensation. The body and mind and emotions beg for relief. When we are in intense pain, our perceptions change. The ways that we see and understand people, places, and time change. A minute may feel like an eternity. Friends or family who do not give us the needed medications to relieve our pain may look like enemies. The hospital room may stare at us like prison walls.

Suffering changes the way that we see life. A heart attack often causes us to see just how white salt actually is, or to notice the orange sunset against the blue sky or that our children are almost grown. After a major illness or severe injury, some people appreciate life more. Their family, friends, and other values are appreciated more. Then there are those who are wounded so severely that life changes radically. Novel character Ishmael Chambers was wounded in the war, both physically and emotionally. He lost an arm, saw buddies killed, and experienced the trauma of seeing the mangled bodies of his friends–alive one moment and in pieces the next. When he returned to San Piedro Island, he settled into a life of journalism, publishing a small newspaper. Ishmael was now different from the young man who left to go to war. David Guterson, author of *Snow Falling on Cedars,* gives us a grim picture of Ishmael:

He had a chip on his shoulder: it was sort of a black joke he shared with himself, a double entendre, made silently. He didn't like many people anymore and very many things, either. He preferred not to be this way, but there it was, he was like that. His cynicism—a veteran's cynicism—disturbed him all the time. It seemed to him after the war that the world was thoroughly altered...In the context of this, much of what went on in normal life seemed wholly and disturbingly ridiculous...The strange thing was, he wanted to like everyone. He just couldn't find a way to do it...He loved humankind dearly and with all his heart, but he disliked most human beings.[2]

Many people who experience intense suffering and look death in the face often experience a radical change in their values. These victims of trauma are sometimes impatient with people who argue over the color to paint the fellowship hall in the church or the hymns that are sung during Sunday worship.

I read someplace that "cynicism is the weapon of the wounded." The trauma causing the suffering may damage our capacity to feel for others, to have compassion for those who hurt in different ways. Milan Kundera, the Czechoslovakian author, speaks to this when he writes, "*I think, therefore I am* is the statement of an intellectual who underrates toothaches. *I feel, therefore I am* is a truth much more universally valid, and it applies to everything that's alive." He claims, "In intense suffering the world disappears and each of us is alone with his suffering; suffering is the university of egocentrism."[3] Of course, we cannot suffer for others, as most parents would like to when their children are in pain, but we can suffer *with* them. Most people suffer with others, and their suffering affects those near to them. The following incident describes a person who was deprived of the capacity to feel for others.

At Lexington Theological Seminary, I was teaching a class to help ministers understand the different ways society affects people and the responses of these people to the world. One of the students in the class knew someone who worked in the criminal justice system. With the help of this student, we invited a man who was out on parole to attend the class and tell his story.

John said, "I killed my first man when I was fourteen years old. I hit him in the head with a large rock." Further questioning revealed that he had killed three people and was on parole after serving time for shooting a man while previously out on parole. In the hour that we questioned him, we got a picture of a society that did not fit our image of the polite people with whom we usually lived and worked.

"How did you feel when you killed that man and watched him lie there bleeding?" I asked.

He looked at me as if confused.

"I don't understand what you're asking," he replied.

"I just want to know if you felt sorry for the man."

"I could kill you right now and never miss a bite of this sandwich...Is that what you mean?"

The expression on John's face was cold. It sent chills through everyone in the room. While growing up, John had been repeatedly beaten and abused in many ways by his father and mother. So he decided that life was too painful to risk any feeling at all. This was not a conscious decision; it was a reaction to constant physical and emotional suffering.

People who do not feel for those who are suffering are handicapped emotionally. Because they cannot feel for others, they cannot hurt with them. As we see in *Snow Falling On Cedars,* Ishmael's inability to empathize with others also diminished his capacity to enjoy others–to celebrate with them when they had occasion for celebration, such as the birth of a child. Ishmael's cynicism kept him focused on what was wrong with others, instead of on seeing what was right. He constantly stared at blemishes and missed the beauty of people. Ishmael wanted to feel for others, to care about what they were doing and saying, but he thought people were too shallow in their thoughts. What they thought was important was not really important in the larger scheme of things that included suffering and dying. Ishmael's capacity for compassion closed down.

Compassion is a gift–a valuable gift. After I had my first angina attack, the cardiologist prescribed Valium. I took one tablet and almost went into an emotional coma. It occurred to me that I did not really care much about anything. I knew that I loved my family, but it seemed more an academic issue than an emotional commitment. I felt as though my response to one of my children running in front of an automobile would be, "I sure hope the car doesn't hit Philip." I was a spectator of life, an emotional zombie. That was the last Valium I ever took. I chose to be in danger of my Type-A behavior's causing a heart attack rather than to live a stoic life drained of passion. This is not to criticize those who benefit from taking tranquilizers. They are evidently helpful to millions of people. Many people function with compassion while taking the prescribed drug. Some people act compassionately only when on medication.

Roscoe Pierson, an exceptionally intelligent person and former librarian at Lexington Theological Seminary, was one of the most interesting people I have ever met. Roscoe never tried to be politically correct. He said what he thought when he thought it. He frequently warned those listening to him, "If you see someone coming to help you, run for your life." Roscoe thought that people who felt they had to help others could do more harm than good. He was afraid of people who wore their acts of compassion as a badge of honor, who practiced their piety on people in pain. These people demonstrate their concern with cookies, a ride to the doctor's office, a listening ear, and other acts that seem to meet the needs of people who need to be helped in these ways. They receive satisfaction from doing for others. They tell others about their deeds, describing their acts of compassion. These people feel good about themselves. They like themselves because they live what they believe. They are who they want to be. In most cases, this compassion is not forced or coerced. It is voluntary; these people are doing for others out of a desire to help. Because some of these people want to be admired for putting their religious faith into action does not discredit their deeds. The motivation that drives a person to act compassionately also tells who the person is; it reveals the character of the person. We do not, nor can we, know all the forces that cause a person to sacrifice for the sake of others. Most people do not know why they do what they do. So we accept their deeds as demonstrations of compassion; at least, most people do.

As physical pain is the "gift nobody wants," emotional pain is the gift some people want and do not have, and others have and do not want. Some people prefer numbness to the pain of caring. At times we may be tempted to give up trying to stop the hurting, to attempt to close down our caring for others who are suffering. Our empathy may overwhelm us. Let us be thankful for the gift of compassion, which enables us to feel deeply for and with others in the spirit of God and to do something about it.

Responses to Specific Instances of Suffering: Alzheimer's Disease and Hospice

Chapter 20

Alzheimer's Disease: A Challenge to Compassion

A few years ago, John Cavendish, a clergyman from Lexington, was traveling through Europe in a rental car when he became sleepy. It was late at night, so he pulled into a rest stop and fell asleep in his car. He awakened to a knock on the car window, a bright light shined in his face, and two law enforcement officers stared in at him. When he lowered the window, the officers questioned him. What was he doing there? What was his destination? Where had he come from? After being satisfied that John was not a criminal, they explained that at the previous rest stop an elderly woman had been abandoned. She did not know who she was or where she came from. There was no way the officers could identify her. John asked about such incidents, and the officers explained that Europe has an epidemic of elderly people being abandoned.

When adult children can no longer take care of their aging, forgetful parents; when they realize how much they have neglected their own children; and when they discover how tired and irritable they have become, some despairing adult children in many countries abandon their parents in one way or another.

In years past, it was not uncommon for grown children to abandon their parents when they became too troublesome, too demanding, and too irritable. These caregivers felt the helplessness of their situation. The medical field could not promise anything but more of the same; they could not promise them a less demanding future. It was depressing to watch a loved one gradually fade into a world that seemed to erase a lifetime of loyalty and love. In despair, the adult children gave up and acted in a way that caused them to feel ashamed for the rest of their lives; they abandoned the one that had given them life. What could they do? This obligation was squeezing the life and love out of them. Many people were being hurt by the situation. Spouses, children, grandchildren, and others were being neglected because grandfather, grandmother, brother, or sister was suffering from Alzheimer's disease. Is this a hopeless situation? No!

The Alzheimer's Disease International Conference has been held for the past twelve years. More than one hundred countries cooperate in an effort to address the many issues that this distressful disease raises. The Twelfth Alzheimer's Disease Conference was held in Jerusalem with the theme "To Give You a Future and a Hope" (Jeremiah 29:11). Those committed to meeting the challenges of Alzheimer's disease focused on what they have in common: people suffering with an illness that first needs understanding, then a cure. These people know what it is to see someone they love gradually lose the gift of memory and the richness of their religious and cultural history. Because such experts gather together to seek solutions to this draining disease, there is hope.

Several years ago I attended a conference on Alzheimer's disease. It was shocking to think about "losing" my mind, becoming so dependent on others, and possibly being hateful to those I love.

"Is there any way for me to know when I am in the early stages of Alzheimer's disease?" I asked Dr. William Markesbery, the director of the University of Kentucky Center on Aging. "No!" he replied. Then he explained the challenge of discovering an earlier diagnosis of the disease.

Fifteen years ago those interested in the disease thought that victims of Alzheimer's disease were "out of touch" before they or anyone else knew they had the disease. The medical approach was, "Keep them dry, warm, and fed." It was a helpless situation. We were condemned to watch the person we loved deteriorate before our eyes. There was not anything we could do to change the frightening future. Now, a few years later, there is more awareness of the disease early in its progression. Years ago if we were the one with Alzheimer's disease, we were not aware that we were going to become dependent and burdensome. Now we may discover that we have the disease before we are out of touch with our world, and some medications show promise of slowing the disease's progression, but there is still not anything that anyone can do that will stop the deterioration of the minds of those who have Alzheimer's disease, at least at the time of this writing.

Now we can become more aware of the disease in our lives. It has been and still is in our midst in the everyday activities of life. The family of a parishioner shunned their minister when the parishioner died. He was asked not to attend the funeral. The minister could not understand. He had visited Mary time and time again and had prayed weekly with her in her home and in the hospital. He spent many hours sitting at her kitchen table, eating cake and drinking coffee, listening to Mary tell stories about her early life. But when Mary's family came to visit her, she told them that she hardly knew the minister because he never visited her. The family did not recognize that Mary had a faulty memory. Sometimes when the memory goes, there is much misunderstanding and suffering, and no one is to blame.

According to an article in *Time,* one out of five families does not recognize the symptoms of Alzheimer's disease (memory loss and confusion) in a loved one. Yet most people have experiences with individuals who have Alzheimer's disease. At the time of such experiences, they may think the person's rudeness, coldness, hostility, or irrational behavior is personal. "It doesn't make sense. How could mother say such a thing to me? She really hurt my feelings." "Why is father so distant? He acts as if he doesn't care that I've been sick."

Even when people know that a loved one has dementia in one form or another, it is still difficult to accept insensitive behavior. Although the person may not be physically abusive, the verbal attacks or being treated like strangers can hurt. It does not seem possible that our mother or father or spouse or friend could be so different.

Sally said, "I have to try to remember who she used to be. This is my mother, who is basically a caring person. No! I said that wrong. Mother is still who she has always been, but now she isn't acting as she used to because she is ill. It's so confusing."

There is hope. Announcements of important Alzheimer's disease research results are being made regularly. As this was being written, there was such an announcement by Dr. William Markesbery. Recent research suggests that for someone who already has the disease but is still functioning relatively well, the added stress of one or more small strokes in strategic areas of the brain can speed the onset of the crippling dementia that ultimately kills the person. Preventing strokes in older people might help potential victims postpone the process of this disease's developing. Lowering blood pressure, quitting smoking, and controlling diabetes are some of the steps that might stem the onset of the disease.[1]

In his book *My Journey Into Alzheimer's Disease,* Robert Davis describes his experience of the illness. Davis was the minister of one of the largest Presbyterian congregations in the United States in the 1980s. His intelligence and organizational abilities were an accepted fact; he knew how to communicate and motivate. A few months after being diagnosed with Alzheimer's disease he wrote:

> I can no longer remember a list that goes above five items. I sometimes become confused and lost even in familiar stores. I can no longer read even such simple things as long magazine articles. I can become lost in a motel room and not even be able to find the door to the bathroom. All mathematical skills are gone. My mind has become a sieve that can only catch and hold certain random things. My IQ has dropped in half.[2]

To read this is frightening to all people and especially to those of us who enjoy ideas, playing with propositions, studying theological systems, and creating concepts. It sends chills through ministers, church leaders, and other people to think about not being able to recite the ritual or to partake of the eucharist ("Do this in memory of me"), to believe and explain biblical concepts, or to confess that Jesus was born, lived, died, and was resurrected. What happens when we cannot remember? Is clear thinking a sign of religious superiority? Do we have some kind of gnostic knowledge stored in our minds that assures us of salvation? If so, what happens when we "lose our minds"?

There is hope. Virginia Bell and David Troxel help us to understand the world of Alzheimer's disease. They give us creative, practical ways to respond to this very complex disease. We can improve the quality of life for people suffering with Alzheimer's disease and their caregivers' lives as well. *The Best Friends Approach to Alzheimer's Care* is a ray of hope for all of us. While the major emphasis is on the things we can do to help the one suffering from Alzheimer's disease, the book is based on sound theological presuppositions.

Bell and Troxel enter into the lives of persons with Alzheimer's disease and their caregivers. They describe the effects the disease has on the entire caring community. They demonstrate how we can be more than a conditioned reflex to the disease and its victims. Their theory is that we must relate to the person as one with infinite value, no matter how immobile they become mentally and physically, and we must treat the disease. There is a major difference in their approach when compared with those of many others who are working with the challenges presented by Alzheimer's disease. Bell and Troxel remind us that by always relating to the person and treating the disease, we can be bearers of hope and help.

First, they share a description of the life of an Alzheimer's patient. The authors remind us that to a person with Alzheimer's, once familiar territory feels like a hostile enemy environment. Alzheimer's disease patients are in a foreign land all the time, and they do not know the language. They experience culture shock in their own backyard. This is what happened to Rebecca Riley:

> Rebecca Riley suspected that she had Alzheimer's disease when she began having difficulty in her teaching. She described her early experience as follows: "Depression, can't say what I want, afraid I can't express my thoughts and words—thus I remain silent and become depressed, I need conversation to be slow, it is

difficult to follow conversation with so much noise, I feel people turn me off because I cannot express myself, I dislike social workers, nurses, and friends who do not treat me as a real person, it is difficult to live one day at a time."[3]

Common feelings and emotions of persons with Alzheimer's disease are a sense of loss, isolation and loneliness, sadness, confusion, worry and anxiety, frustration, fear, paranoia, anger, and embarrassment. How each of these emotions affects both the people with Alzheimer's disease and their caregivers is described. Bell and Troxel remind us that as the person loses social contacts, and when friends stop visiting, emotions bubble up to compound the problems. These people are not stupid or ignorant; they suffer from a disabling disease. As one person put it, "There are too many used-tos in my life now. I used to remember names, addresses, and where my wallet was."

With more than thirty-six years of combined experience working with persons with dementia, Bell and Troxel are especially insightful in describing ways of responding to Alzheimer's disease. They write: "We cannot choose whether someone develops the disease, but we can choose how we will respond to the illness and whether it will bring our family together or drive it apart."[4] A critical contribution by Bell and Troxel is the emphasis on the positive parts of the life of a person who suffers from Alzheimer's disease. Most of what we read laments the losses—the loss of mobility and memory, the loss of control in one's life, the loss of skills (tying shoestrings or reading a long paragraph), and others. Their book teaches us to focus on that which is left—the strengths and abilities that can still give a person pride, pleasure, and a sense of identity.

The foundation for this approach is "An Alzheimer's Disease Bill of Rights," which follows:

- To be informed of one's diagnosis.
- To have appropriate, ongoing medical care.
- To be productive in work and play for as long as possible.
- To be treated like an adult, not like a child.
- To have expressed feelings taken seriously.

- To be free from psychotropic medications, if possible.
- To live in a safe, structured, and predictable environment.
- To enjoy meaningful activities that fill each day.
- To be outdoors on a regular basis.
- To have physical contact, including hugging, caressing, and handholding.
- To be with individuals who know one's life story, including cultural and religious traditions.
- To be cared for by individuals who are well trained in dementia care.[5]

Two concepts are offered that are especially helpful and hopeful in making a difference in the lives of those suffering from Alzheimer's disease.

First, the concept of friendship is fundamental when relating to persons with Alzheimer's disease. Elements of friendship can teach us much about Alzheimer's care. Such elements include knowing each other's backgrounds and traditions, understanding individual personalities, doing things together, initiating activities, providing encouragement, building self-esteem, listening well, giving compliments, asking opinions, enjoying old stories, laughing together, having a sense of equality, living with the ups and downs, and, above all, working at the relationship.

Second, friendship works because people have and learn the "knack" for relating to friends who have Alzheimer's. This includes family members and professional workers in care facilities. Several examples of "knack" and "no-knack" are described so that caregivers may discover how to give and to receive a ray of hope in situations that feels hopeless. Elements of knack include the following:

- Being well-informed
- Having empathy
- Respecting the basic rights of the person
- Maintaining caregiving integrity
- Communicating skillfully
- Maintaining optimism
- Setting realistic expectations
- Using humor

- Maintaining patience
- Developing flexibility
- Being nonjudgmental
- Maintaining self-confidence
- Taking care of oneself
- Planning ahead

Caregivers cannot maintain such care at all times; that would require compassion of a divine nature. Yet there are times when caregivers mirror God by loving the person in an understanding and accepting way in word and deed.

Chapter 21

Alzheimer's Disease: A Theological Reflection

Alzheimer's disease tests our patience and faith. It may threaten the hope we need when someone we love deteriorates mentally and physically. "When confronted by the dissolution and suffering of Alzheimer's disease, it is forgiveness and, ultimately, the promise of the resurrection which allow us to rejoice," claims David Keck,[1] a church historian whose mother had Alzheimer's disease. Keck does not believe that the resurrection is a "pie in the sky" concept in which we do not have to worry about anything while trying to pretend that others and we are not really suffering. Suffering is not just a little inconvenience that we have to put up with until Jesus returns to take us to heaven.

In *Forgetting Whose We Are: Alzheimer's Disease and the Love of God,* Keck leads us through sin and suffering to forgiveness that helps us keep our sanity through the month-by-month, week-by-week, day-by-day, and yes, minute-by-minute demands of this disease that sometimes cause us to lose patience and secretly think thoughts that would not stand the test of polite company. Keck offers the theological foundation for doing what we believe. He writes:

> Important advice abounds, but where is the rich spiritual reflection and penetrating counseling? Clearly, our family is confronting a lethal disease that drains my

127

mother of her memories and identity and us of strength. Clearly, this disease is raising profound challenges about who we are and how we might relate to God as well as to each other. Clearly, we are called to remember what God is doing in all of this.[2]

Keck's book is a sensitive treatment of the problems facing us as we ask such questions as: What happens when one cannot confess the creeds, recite the rituals, or remember the meaning of baptism or the purpose of the eucharist? What does the church say to the victims of Alzheimer's disease and their families? While Keck's book primarily addresses theological issues, there are gems of practical advice that come from a person whose mother had Alzheimer's disease.

Whereas the practical advice is helpful, the hope we find in Keck's words is in the God of the past, present, and future. He proclaims that orthodoxy, defined broadly as being faithful to the creeds and ecumenical councils, is crucial because it describes the framework within which we can proceed confidently with faith, hope, and love. We will view the Christian caregiver's relationship and responsibility to the patient as Keck describes the dynamic. He points out that caregivers should realize the limits of their care, be humbled by their limitations, and accept their roles as stewards while admitting that they will not change the basic condition of the patient. Although they cannot change the deteriorating effects of the disease and the sometimes rapid loss of the patient's control of most aspects of his or her life, they can see in the resurrection a hope for the future. Christian caregivers may come to believe that they will see their spouses, parents, grandparents, or other loved ones in the future in much better condition. Keck reminds us, "In Pauline terms…when we hug each other at the Resurrection, we will be 'face to face' with those who were once demented, and their faces will be radiant with knowledge and love."[3]

He advises: "A family witnessing the dissolution of a loved one does not need careful intellectual conceptualization, but a person saying without hesitation, 'Yes, it is true! God so loved the world that he gave his only son for our sakes so that we might have eternal life.'"[4] Believing in the confession makes the future a part of the present situation. The future is a significant presence in our lives today, and that presence can affect how we feel and respond to our loved ones who have been damaged by the dementing disease.

However, until the eschaton (the end times—death and the resurrection) arrives, we will have to deal with much in our emotions and behaviors that dampen our hope for that future. We may have to survive the loss of

- a full night's sleep,
- a hot cup of coffee,
- a day to shop for groceries without feeling that we have to rush home,
- an evening at the theater or a nice restaurant without feeling guilty, and
- the chance to retrieve that unkind word spoken in frustration or anger.

The absence of the simple rituals of life does not make it easy to feel good about or find hope in the future.

Acedia is a condition all caregivers experience. It is described as weariness in welldoing. When exhaustion overcomes caregivers, they sometimes do and say things of which they feel ashamed. The guilt feelings and anger evoked by the seemingly endless demands of caring compound the burden on one who wants to do what is best for the victim of Alzheimer's disease. "For caregivers, feelings of failure are almost inevitable…The wickedness of our thoughts and behavior strikes us in the depths of our being and our ugliness becomes overwhelming…The *acedia* of care giving is real, and the awful effects on the soul are profound. But so, too, are the Cross and the resurrection real and so, too, are their effects on the soul beyond measure."[5] Keck leads us through sin and suffering to forgiveness that helps us keep our sanity in the midst of the draining demands of this disease.

Duree is the idea of the past making itself known in the present. A song, a name, a sunset, a verse of scripture, or a particular incident may evoke images and feelings that are a part of us. It is our past breaking into our lives at any moment to live again in us. Religious history is a valuable resource for retaining the richness of who we were and whom we enjoy being. Hymns bring back feelings of joy and salvation. A picture of Jesus may bring tears of joy to one who can hardly remember her or his own name. The patient with Alzheimer's disease not only remembers the incident, but feels the depth of religious assurance. He or she may feel the comfort of a lifelong friendship like the one Mary affirmed at the birth of her first child. The patient is overcome with awesome feelings at seeing and holding her or his first grandchild. The caregiver administers the special events stored in the memory of the patient. Keck and Bell and Troxel stress the importance of knowing and using the personal history of the loved one to minister to one who might not remember much about what is happening today, but can still celebrate life as it comes out of the past.

Keck's interpretation of prayer, the church, and the use of *duree* in living with patients challenges us to attempt to do the same with our theology. The following are a few quotations to ignite our imagination.

- "The resurrected Lord whose life was given on the Cross because God so loved the world is with us. Prayers are answered, grace is recognized in the soul, and the peace that passes understanding is bestowed."[6]
- "Whenever we struggle against the ever-threatening victory of sin and death, such as when we become caregivers, we participate properly in the work of God."[7]
- "Through the *duree* of Christian memories, we feel the power of God's merciful presence."[8]
- "Praying for someone is perhaps the finest way to remember a person."[9]

This is an all-too-brief introduction to Keck's application of Orthodox theology to the problems and challenges of Alzheimer's disease. Readers are encouraged to examine their own and Keck's theology as it speaks to the victims of Alzheimer's disease and their caregivers.

"The cross and the basic beliefs of the church teach us that instead of explaining our suffering, God shares it."[10] Above all else remember: There is hope! We can pray with gratitude:

Our eternal God, we are thankful that even when we do not and cannot remember you, you and your caregivers remember us with grace and love. In the name of the one who promised your presence and peace, Jesus the Christ, we pray. Amen.

Chapter 22

Hospice: God's Compassion

Hospice began in London in 1967 at St. Christopher's Hospital. When visitors ask how St. Christopher's hospice began, they are told the story of a young Pole who was dying of cancer in another London hospital. "There ought to be a better way to take care of people in your condition," a nurse said to him one day. When the young man died, he left his savings of more than one thousand dollars to begin a fund to start a hospice for the terminally ill. He said to the nurse, "I will be your window in such a building." A staff member of St. Christopher's said, "With that as a start, we had no choice but to go ahead and create a place where patients could be surrounded with a more pleasant life."[1]

Many years later we read the words of the Reverend Colette Horan:

> Early in our ministry, my husband, Dana, and I served as hospice chaplains in Ashland, Kentucky, the small community in which we lived. We never dreamed at that time that hospice would be there for us in our time of need.
>
> I found hospice so helpful because the hospice people had the same goals for Dana that he and I did. He wanted to be at home to die and he wanted to be as comfortable as possible. Our hospice caregivers resonated immediately to those specific goals. They gave Dana, me, and our extended family excellent,

compassionate care. They were present, but not intrusive. They were tender, yet firm, when decisions had to be made. They provided information for any questions I asked and tried to help me do whatever I thought best. It was a great relief to know that I could depend on them.

We had co-team leaders. They were to alternate visits. As time progressed, they each came every day. They each told me not to tell the other one of the extra visit. When I asked them why they were both coming, the answer was, "We both love Dana and like to be around if either of you needs us."

Since my husband and I both were ordained ministers, we decided to ask hospice not to provide the chaplain services. We had a large number of clergy friends who were very supportive. The team was very flexible and understood our desires and request.

Reverend Horan understands the hospice approach to suffering. She experienced the depth of compassion as she cared for others in the program. She also received compassion from caring, sensitive people in the hospice program when she needed special help dealing with Dana's illness and death.

Hospice provides a creative and compassionate response to suffering. Although the idea that we should relate compassionately to people suffering is not new, hospice is one of the most holistic programs ever developed. It addresses the basic needs of people who are dying and their caregivers. Hospice shows us that dying does not have to be an impersonal process of perpetuating pain and fracturing families with frantic feats of medical heroics. We can die with dignity and without senseless suffering.

Parker Rossman captures our fears when he writes:

As many people contemplate death, many of them fear isolation and pain. They worry that unnecessary and uncomfortable treatments will continue after being no longer necessary, thus diminishing the quality of life and family associations in their last days. They only have to visit the wards of almost any hospital to see people taped down, plugged into machines, isolated from grandchildren and pets, lonely and in miserable circumstances. The real fear of death for many persons therefore is a dread of loss of control of their life, of not even being consulted when crucial decisions are made between alternatives of treatment and care.[2]

There is the fear that we will have to endure excruciating physical pain when there is no hope for curing the cause of the pain. Hospice addresses this and other issues with compassion. The hospice approach includes the following principles:

- The setting for dying is a place where patients are surrounded with people who care what they think, feel, want, fear, and love. Caregivers take time to listen and share life in a dignified way.
- The patient is respected and, if at all possible, all wishes are met.
- When possible, patients are surrounded with personal items, including family, friends, pets, chairs, tables from home, favorite clothes, music, pictures, and are given their favorite foods to eat. (A Big Mac and fries may be a real gift to a teenager or senior citizen who is dying.)
- Hospice programs supply medical, psychological, and spiritual services. Doctors, nurses, social workers, counselors, religious advisers, and volunteer workers try to meet every need possible as they work closely with families of dying patients.

Allen Lee Holsopple reminds us that "spiritual counselors may be able to point the way to the eradication of guilt, regret, bitterness, and other hostile feelings or so enable the patient to gain courage to talk about his/her anger toward people and God, and thus achieve an inner sense of forgiveness and peace, which makes the dying process easier for all involved."[3]

Dr. Cicely Saunders says, "A mature and sensitive minister can be of invaluable help as the patient prepares for his or her death and tries to understand its relation to his or her faith or philosophy of life…The sacraments can become practical and powerful vehicles of God's concern for those who suffer."[4]

Thelma Ingles captures the essence of the hospice program when she writes:

> The patient who is dying wants freedom from pain, yet not the dulling of awareness that interferes with his relationships with others. He wants friendliness and kindness and the comforting measures that tell him he is still important...And above all, he wants to be assured that when his time comes, those who have been close to him will remember him with love and respect.[5]

Hospice tries to do all that for people who have less than six months to live and who accept the fact that the last months, weeks, and days can be times of celebration and joy as people share life in a loving way.

A few months after Dana's death, Colette wrote:

> *The cold fingers of death curled*
> *a hand in yours and drew you away*
> *your spirit soared to a new*
> *dwelling place and I am left*
> *seeking the meaning of new life.*
> *My faith seems to be secure in*
> *my head even if not always*
> *felt in my heart—*
> *In the empty spaces, time lingers,*
> *and suspends.*
>
> *The healing must take place from*
> *within—carefully sewn with*
> *deliberate stitches. If even a*
> *particle is left untreated it could*
> *delay the new growth.*
> *And the tears come and come*
> *and come—but what do they wash*
> *away? Nothing—but the flood*
> *subsides and the tender balance*
> *again weighs in.*

Suffering is our emotional response to pain. Although there are different ways we respond to our own and others' suffering, and what is helpful to one person may not be to another, some actions are helpful to almost all people—a kind word, a caring touch, a brief prayer, a piece of chocolate pie, a video of their favorite sport or movie, and most importantly, a listening ear that lures others to believe that *God and we care.*

After all, suffering is a community affair. We do not have to suffer alone. We share our sufferings and joys with one another through churches and organizations created to care, thereby becoming the people we were created to become.

Resources for Those Dying and Their Caregivers

All hospice services are not the same; they vary from community to community, region to region, and nation to nation. So when you are in need of the services of hospice, investigate to find out what is available and the quality of services offered.[6] For information contact:

- Your local hospice offices or the National Hospice and Palliative Care Organization at 1-800-658-8898. Web site: www.nhpco.org.
- Hospice Foundation of America, which furnishes brochures on how to select a hospice or how to be a hospice volunteer. Call 1-800-854-3402. Web site: www.hospicefoundation.org.

Postscript

I Still Rebel…

On November 5, 2000, my friend Karen shared her wisdom again. Here are her words describing her continuing responses to suffering.

I had a treatment today, and my regular chemo nurse wasn't there. The nurse who treated me said, "How long have you been doing this?" "Six years," I answered. Six years since the day I found out I was terminally ill. For a dying woman, I'm doing awfully well. I *do* have some after-effects of cancer and treatment. One of those is that I cannot work in a full-time ministry; I live on disability, and work part-time to supplement that income. Since treatment I've pastored two churches and taught two semesters at Vanderbilt. These days I'm writing a screenplay and spending as much time as possible in clay up to my elbows, pursuing a talent I didn't know I had: sculpture. I spend every spare minute laughing with those dear, loyal friends who stuck by me through my ordeal and have become my family. Once a week, I take out the garbage.

Very soon after it looked like I might hang around awhile, I started pestering God. Now that I had received my miracle, I wanted to know why I had been saved. I figured there simply had to be a purpose to my continued existence. Surely there was a grand mission I was to complete. Nothing seemed obvious. I spent several years as a sort of cancer "poster girl," being interviewed for the newspaper and magazines, and speaking at fund-raisers for the Vanderbilt Ingram Cancer Center. Even those days have passed, though; my story is old news.

I am to this day ready for the big mission should it come, but I suspect I have finally figured out what's going on. I could well be wrong, but I don't think there will be a special call to do something heroic or spectacular. I think God has simply given to me the gift she has given to all of us: the gift of life. All we're expected to do in return is to live it, savoring each and every moment, sucking the marrow out of its bones—and to take out the trash when we have to.

Six years of being terminally ill. At what point does the diagnosis cease to have meaning? I don't believe any more that I'm going to be dead in six months, but I'm also not worrying about retirement. I think about death each and every day, and as time has gone on, I have become more accustomed to the idea.

Death I can handle; it's the suffering I still rebel against. There *are* things worse than death. Looking back on the period when I suffered, I think it makes sense that all I wanted in the midst of it was for it to stop. With the luxury of time, though, I can see it differently. Anyone who can welcome suffering with open arms is an ascended master, as far as I'm concerned. But given that we all must suffer at some time or another, it seems important to remember that no matter how horrible the suffering, God *will* bring something good out of it. I will never like suffering—not for myself or anyone else, and I reserve the right to complain loudly in the midst of it. But I have come to the point where I can allow that in the great, grand scheme of things, it has some purpose. It is not meaningless.

Still. There will come a day when my dear, beloved oncologist will have to say to me, "It's active again." And he will lay out for me all my treatment options. If I'm lucky, there will be something new and wonderful that I can take and go on with my life. If I'm not lucky, and the options are as they exist today…well, then, I plan to enjoy the hell out of the last six months of my life. It will be a choice between kinds of suffering then: the suffering of death, or the suffering of unending chemotherapy. I know most people think death is the worse of the two. But I'm a Christian, and I know it has a mighty reward on the other side. I love life so much I can barely tell you, but if it's time, I'm ready to go home. I'm just hoping the invitation doesn't come for a good long while.

Notes

Chapter 1: Levels of Suffering

[1]Gavin de Becker, *The Gift of Fear* (New York: Little, Brown, and Company, 1997), 48.
[2]Frederick Buechner, "The Dwarves in the Stable," in *Listening for God,* ed. Paula J. Carlson and Peter S. Hawkins (Minneapolis: Augsburg, 1994), 39.
[3]Ibid., 50.
[4]Ibid., 39.
[5]Elie Wiesel, *Twilight,* trans. Marion Wiesel (New York. Summit Books, 1987), 213.

Chapter 2: Radical Suffering

[1]Wendy Farley, *Tragic Vision and Divine Compassion* (Louisville: Westminster/John Knox Press, 1990), 53.
[2]Primo Levi, *The Drowned and The Saved* (New York: Vintage Press, 1989), 75.
[3]Darrell Fasching, *Narrative Theology After Auschwitz* (Minneapolis: Augsburg/Fortress, 1992), 48.
[4]Dorothee Soelle, *Suffering,* trans. Everett R. Kalin (Philadelphia: Fortress Press, 1973), 85.
[5]Milan Kundera, *Immortality,* trans. Peter Kussi (New York: Harper Perennial, 1992), 200.

Chapter 3: No Pain, No Gain

[1]Steve Wulf, "Faster, Higher, Braver," *Time* 149, no. 7 (August 5, 1996): 32.
[2]John Worthen, *D. H. Lawrence* (New York: Martin's Press, 1989), 70.
[3]Ibid., 71.
[4]Ibid., 54.
[5]Ibid., 77.

Chapter 4: The Gift of Pain

[1]Paul Brand and Philip Yancey, *Pain: The Gift Nobody Wants* (New York: HarperCollins, 1993), 5.
[2]Ibid., 12.
[3]Ibid., 201.
[4]Albert Camus, *Notebooks 1942–1951,* trans. Justin O'Brien (New York: Harcourt Brace Jovanovich, 1965), 67.
[5]Simone Weil, *Waiting For God,* trans. Emma Craufurd (New York: Putnam, 1951), 118.
[6]Kaye Gibbons, *Sights Unseen* (New York: G. P. Putnam's Sons, 1995), 4.
[7]David Morris, *The Culture of Pain* (Berkeley: University of California Press, 1993), 143.
[8]Brand and Yancey, *Pain: The Gift Nobody Wants,* 17.
[9]Chinua Achebe, *Things Fall Apart* (New York: Doubleday, 1959).

Chapter 5: Fear as Suffering

[1]Dorothy Fosdick, *The International Dictionary of Thoughts: An Encyclopedia of Quotations from Every Age for Every Occasion,* comp. John P. Bradley, Leo F. Daniels, and Thomas C. Jones (Chicago: J.G. Ferguson Publishing Company, 1969), 288.
[2]Edward Burke, *The International Dictionary of Thoughts,* 288.

[3]William Burham, *The International Dictionary of Thoughts,* 288.
[4]Susan Jeffers, *Feel The Fear and Do Away With It* (New York: Fawcett Columbine, 1987), 28.
[5]Dorothy Thompson, *The International Dictionary of Thoughts,* 290.
[6]Gavin de Becker, *The Gift of Fear* (New York: Little, Brown and Company, 1997), 19.
[7]Ibid., 21.

Chapter 6: Pray!

[1]Response to the questionnaire during a seminar at Lexington Theological Seminary.
[2]Thomas H. Green, S.J., *Darkness in the Marketplace* (Notre Dame: Ave Maria Press, 1981), 82.

Chapter 7: Our Prayers Reveal Who We Are

[1]Sharyn Echols Dowd, *Prayer, Power, and The Problem Of Suffering* (Atlanta: Scholars Press, 1986), 144.
[2]William O. Paulsell, *Rules For Prayer* (New York: Paulist Press, 1993), 113.
[3]Jimmy Breslin, *I Want to Thank My Brain for Remembering Me* (New York: Little, Brown, and Company, 1996), 6.
[4]Ibid., 6–7.
[5]Paulsell, *Rules for Prayer,* 89.
[6]Dietrich Bonhoeffer, *The Cost of Discipleship* (New York: Touchstone, 1995), 16.
[7]Paulsell, *Rules for Prayer,* 87.
[8]Ibid., 92.
[9]Ibid., 135.
[10]Larry Dossey, *Prayer Is Good Business* (San Francisco: Harper San Francisco, 1996), 142.

Chapter 8: Finding God in Prayer

[1]Edward M. Hallowell and John J. Ratey, *Driven to Distraction* (New York: Simon & Schuster, 1994).
[2]Norman Vincent Peale, *The Power of Positive Thinking* (New York: Fawcett, 1952).
[3]See Marjorie Hewitt Suchocki, *In God's Presence* (St. Louis: Chalice Press, 1996).
[4]Ibid., 61.
[5]Ibid.
[6]Ibid., 63.
[7]Ibid., 66.

Chapter 9: The Variety of Ways of Responding

[1]Kathleen Norris, *Dakota: A Spiritual Journal* (Boston: Houghton Mifflin, 1993), 76–77.

Chapter 10: Blaming the Victim

[1]John Irving, *Trying to Save Piggy Sneed* (New York: Arcade, 1996), 10.
[2]Judith Lewis Herman, *Trauma and Recovery* (New York: Basics Books, 1992), 215.
[3]David B. Morris, *The Culture of Pain* (Los Angeles: University of California Press, 1991), 175.
[4]Ibid., 192, 193.

Chapter 11: Responses That Hurt

[1]Antoinette Bosco, *The Pummeled Heart: Finding God Through Pain* (Mystic, Conn.: Twenty-third Publications, 1994), 86.
[2]Brian Boyd, *Vladimir Nabokov* (Princeton: Princeton Press, 1990), 10.

Chapter 12: Trying to Make Sense of It

[1]C. S. Lewis, *The Problem of Pain* (New York: Collier Books, 1962), 96, 107.
[2]David Polk, ed., *What's a Christian to Do?* (St. Louis: Chalice Press, 1991), 52.
[3]C. S. Lewis, *A Grief Observed* (New York: Bantam Books, 1963), 22.
[4]Ibid., 28.

Chapter 14: The Language of Healing

[1]Susan Kuner, Carol Matzkin Orsborn, Linda Quigley, and Karen Leigh Stroup, *Speaking the Language of Healing* (Berkeley: Conari Press, 1999), xi.
[2]Ibid., 14.

Chapter 15: Which God Do You Choose?

[1]Dorothee Soelle, *Suffering,* trans. Everett R. Kalin (Philadelphia: Fortress Press, 1993), 142.
[2]Leo Rosten, *Life Studies* (New York: St. Martin's Press, 1986), 540.
[3]Quoted in Darrell J. Fashing, *Narrative Theology After Auschwitz* (Minneapolis: Fortress Press, 1992), 57.
[4]Dorothee Soelle, *Suffering,* 155.
[5]David Polk, ed., *What's a Christian to Do?* (St. Louis: Chalice Press, 1991), 65.
[6]Wendy Farley, *Tragic Vision and Divine Compassion* (Louisville: Westminster/ John Knox Press, 1990), 106–14.
[7]Viktor E. Frankl, *Man's Search For Meaning: An Introduction to Logotherapy,* trans. Ilse Lasch (New York: Washington Square Press, 1963), 58–59.

Chapter 16: Compassion 101

[1]Francoise Sagan, *A Fleeting Sorrow,* trans. Richard Seaver (New York: Arcade, 1994).
[2]Raymond Carver, "A Small, Good Thing," in *Cathedral* (New York: Vintage Books, 1981), 59–89.

Chapter 17: God's Endorphin for the Heart

[1]Kaye Gibbons, *A Virtuous Woman* (New York: Vintage Books, 1989), 4.
[2]Week of Compassion Updates on the DiscipleNet, The Christian Church (Disciples of Christ), February 25, 1998.
[3]Dorothee Soelle, *Suffering,* trans. Everett R. Kalin (Philadelphia: Fortress Press, 1993), 142.
[4]Judith Lewis Herman, *Trauma and Recovery* (New York: Basic Books, 1992), 178.
[5]Donald P. McNeill, Douglas A. Morrison, Henry J. M. Nouwen, *Compassion* (New York: Image Books, 1982), 4.

Chapter 18: Warm Hands

[1]Wendy Farley, *Tragic Vision and Divine Compassion* (Louisville: Westminster/John Knox Press, 1990), 73.
[2]David Keck, *Forgetting Whose We Are: Alzheimer's Disease and the Love of God* (Nashville: Abingdon Press, 1996), 161.

[3]William Paulsell, *Tough Minds, Tender Hearts: Six Prophets of Social Justice* (New York: Paulist Press, 1990), 30–35. This book gives a brief synopsis of Weil's life. For additional study, see especially Simone Weil's *Waiting for God* (New York: Putnam's, 1951).

[4]Ibid., 44, 45.

[5]Dorothee Soelle, *Suffering,* trans. Everett R. Kalin (Philadelphia: Fortress Press, 1973), 166.

[6]Untitled news announcement, *Focus,* The University of Florida, vol. 4, no. 2, Spring 1996.

[7]Paul Brand and Philip Yancey, *Pain: The Gift Nobody Wants* (New York: HarperCollins, 1993), 57.

Chapter 19: The Gift of Compassion

[1]David Morris, *The Culture of Pain* (Berkeley: University of California, 1991), 143.

[2]David Guterson, *Snow Falling on Cedars* (New York: Vintage Books, 1995), 35–36.

[3]Milan Kundera, *Immortality,* trans. Peter Kussi (New York: Harper, 1990), 200.

Chapter 20: Alzheimer's Disease: A Challenge to Compassion

[1]"Study: Ibuprofen Cuts Alzheimer's Risk," *The Lexington Herald-Leader,* March 10, 1997.

[2]Robert Davis, *My Journey Into Alzheimer's Disease* (Wheaton, Ill.: Tyndale House, 1989).

[3]Virginia Bell and David Troxel, *The Best Friends Approach to Alzheimer's Care* (Baltimore: Health Professions Press, 1997), 10.

[4]Ibid., 25.

[5]Ibid., 38.

Chapter 21: Alzheimer's Disease: A Theological Reflection

[1]David Keck, *Forgetting Whose We Are: Alzheimer's Disease and The Love of God* (Nashville: Abingdon Press, 1996), 197.

[2]Ibid., 14–15.

[3]Ibid., 154.

[4]Ibid., 85.

[5]Ibid., 165ff.

[6]Ibid., 223.

[7]Ibid., 135.

[8]Ibid., 81.

[9]Ibid., 211.

[10]Ibid., 143.

Chapter 22: Hospice: God's Compassion

[1]Parker Rossman, *Hospice* (New York: Association Press, 1977), 84. Although this information is available in many sources, Rossman describes it succinctly.

[2]Ibid., 20.

[3]Allen Lee Holsopple, "Death From A Hospice Perspective" (master's thesis, Lexington Theological Seminary, 1986), 23.

[4]Quote from Cicely Saunders in *A Hospice Handbook,* ed. Michael P. Hamilton and Helen F. Reid (Grand Rapids: Eerdmans, 1980), xi.

[5]Thelma Ingles, "St. Christopher's Hospice," in *A Hospice Handbook,* ed. Michael P. Hamilton and Helen F. Reid (Grand Rapids: Eerdmans, 1980), 47–48.

[6]See also Denise Glavan, Cindy Longanacre, and John Spivey, *Hospice, A Labor of Love* (St. Louis: Chalice Press, 1999), especially the very useful self-study questionnaire on the personal suitability of hospice care in appendix A, 105–12.